MARTINA GOERNEMANN

SOURDOUGH

FOUR DAYS TO HAPPINESS

PHOTOGRAPHY BY BARBARA SIMON

PRESTEL
Munich – London – New York

CONTENTS

WELCOME

SOURDOUGH IS FOOD FOR THE SOUL!

Hardly a day goes by which isn't too full.

Or too loud. Or doesn't spoil our mood or try our nerves. We're constantly searching for ways to slow down but can't seem to find out how.

Apparently we can only find inner peace through extreme outdoor adventures or perilous yoga asanas. But most of us don't have a tree at our disposal to hug in the evenings and we are usually too tired for downward facing dog.

Many of us have lost our trust that everything will turn out well in the end.

I was looking for a tool to help me get back into balance. No tantric consciousness-expanding exercises or contrast baths. Something simple! Something calming when the world dragged me down ... I'll never forget that it happened to be a Wednesday when I smiled down at a beige-colored blob in a jar. I had discovered sourdough.

Sourdough is more than a homemade baking agent.

Sourdough is a philosophy of life in a jar. It helps us to connect with the best in ourselves. Sourdough emboldens the cautious and fills still waters with pride. It guides us into calm channels when anxiety raises its face and it teaches us not to give up.

My first attempts were a battle!

I wanted to show that sourdough just who's boss of the bowl, but it taught me to give up control and practice patience. With myself and with the sourdough. Sourdough passes through our hands many times. We get to know it like a good friend by the time it turns into bread. The dough is folded, pulled, steamed and sometimes decorated with a design. The loaf that finally rises fills us with pride.

Cultivating sourdough and using it to bake bread is the new "Ommmmm!"

A down-to-earth "Om"! Everybody should have a jar of homemade sourdough living in their fridge and use it to bake as often as possible.

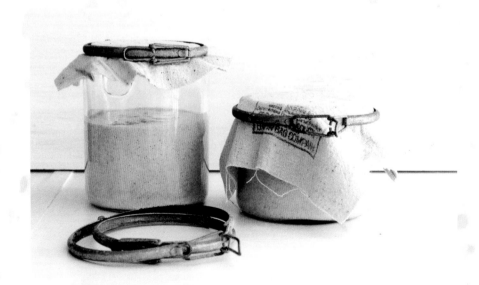

BRING FLOUR AND WATER TO LIFE

In the beginning there was bread. Sourdough bread.
Natural and good. I wanted to bake breads like that. Breads with crunchy crusts and which smelled like heaven. My first setback took place when I learned that sourdough has to get its drive from a sourdough starter. Some recipes mention something called mother dough. I was confused.

Sourdough starters grow in jam jars and are made of flour, water and patience.
I have to thank the internet for this information. Some starters were even passed along from generation to generation. Sourdough could win the hearts of its creator like a house pet. What in the world were they talking about?

I wanted that kind of house pet.
A sourdough starter which I had grown myself. There are many recipes for the cultivation. I chose the 1:1 method. Flour and water is mixed in a 1:1 ratio and poured into a jar. Put in a warm place and fed at the same time on three consecutive days. The starter in the jar is reduced to its original weight each time before flour and water 1:1:1 goes into the next round of feeding.

Organic flour is supposed to simplify the start, I read. I even chose organic whole grain flour which promised to deliver a high performance starter.

Tap water is okay, I learned. Water which contains chlorine is not. I was safe in Munich with its first-class tap water.

My sourdough starter had everything it needed.
It had my full attention and a spot at the window with a view of the garden. The mouth of the jar was lovingly covered with a piece of cloth to allow helpful microbes in the air to enter. And what were my thanks? My new pet just lay around and blubbered listlessly in its jar. I would rather not talk about my first bread.

"That's not going to work,"
I thought, and started experiment number two. I scoured the internet for useful tips and watched countless videos on YouTube. Apparently I had fed and mixed the starter correctly, and it still couldn't motivate itself to help me bake. I decided to send it to sourdough heaven and to mix up a nicer batch. I gazed at its bubbles for the last time … a beautiful pattern. And it even smelled good. Like granola with apples.
Out of flour and water there is life. I just couldn't manage to pour the contents of the jar down the drain. Maybe the sourdough was simply shy? Or extremely cautious?

We needed help.
A personal trainer! I went searching for the cooler I had picked up some time ago at a flea market. It was perfect for transporting the jar and keeping it at a constant temperature. My sourdough starter and I were going on a trip. To Belgium. That's where they have a Sourdough Library and, with some luck, a smart librarian as well.

HAPPINESS MULTIPLIES ITSELF IN FOUR DAYS

St. Vith is a small place.
The Sourdough Library is located on the grounds of a former golf course on the city outskirts. You walk down long hallways and past a bakery gleaming with chrome. This is where new sourdough recipes are tried out. The entire place smells like fresh bread.

The high security, well-tempered bakery is directly next to the Sourdough Library.
You can only enter if you know either the code or Karl De Smedt. The Belgian company Puratos puts a lot of effort into managing the archive. Each sourdough sample has its own compartment and personal history. Every jar is opened regularly; the dough fed and tested for its state of health. Karl De Smedt takes care of the sourdough and travels

around the world looking to acquire special sourdough specimens for the library. He even makes films about the more unusual ones.*
He bakes magnificent breads, speaks six languages and loves sourdough. And because he doesn't just love, but truly knows, everything about sourdough, I can't imagine a better personal trainer for my weakling sourdough starter.

Microorganisms from the air and flour cause the sourdough to bubble, Karl tells me.
They eat the sugar which is found in flour and form acetic acid and lactic acid bacteria. He even paints me pictures of grinning lactic acids and draws a curve which shows the proper ratio of acids. If the starter is namely too cold or too warm, more acetic acids and too few lactic acids are formed or the other way around "and then the starter can't come to life," says Karl.
"I swear, I did everything according to the instructions," I said. Karl laughed, "Give him time. Your starter needs good flour and you need to be patient."

I felt I had been caught out. Patience is not namely one of my virtues.
"Sourdough is a living organism. It is as individual as we are. It's sometimes in a good mood, and sometimes not," Karl said.

Karl talks about sourdough like he would about a friend.
I begin to understand more and more the magic which is hidden in sourdough. As soon as a starter begins to bubble, you also fall in love with it. Throw it down the drain because it's too sluggish? No way! I was happy that I had taken it to Belgium instead and I wasn't going home without hearing all of the good tips for the successful cultivation of a sourdough starter.

Day one:
100 g water plus
100 g flour: Mix together and
allow to rest for 24 hours.

Day two:
200 g starter plus
100 g water plus
120 g flour: Mix together and
allow to rest for 24 hours.

Days three and four:
200 g starter plus
100 g water plus
120 g flour: Mix together and
allow to rest for 24 hours.

The starter that Karl De Smedt mixes generally needs four to seven days before it is ready to be pressed into service.

The temperature at which the sourdough starter grows best should be consistent and between 68 and 95 degrees Fahrenheit. At higher or lower temperatures, the mixture just lies around in its jar and sulks.

The rubber band on the jar is a valuable measuring instrument. It shows whether the starter is ready or not. The rubber band is fastened around the jar on day four after feeding and should mark the upper edge of the dough. As soon as the starter has doubled in bulk within eight hours, it is ready to use in baking.

The testing instruments which we can fully trust are nose and eyes. We can see and smell whether our sourdough starter is doing well. A strong, sour smell means that it is hungry and needs more flour! A green fur cap tells you: Bye bye sourdough! Mold indicates that the mixture is on its way to sourdough heaven.

The consistency of a well-cultivated sourdough starter resembles apple sauce, says Karl. When you scoop a spoonful of starter out of the jar, it should land in the bowl with an elegant plop. It shouldn't pour like a milkshake or land with a slap like a dumpling.

The smell of a ready-to-go sourdough starter should at best call to mind a breakfast granola. Fruity and milky and mildly sour.

The refrigerator is the sourdough starter's favorite place to hang out when it isn't being used. As soon as the starter is ready, this is where it waits for its next assignments. It is fed its 1:1:1 mixture and is taken out to warm up to room temperature.

LONG LIVE THE STARTER!

Once your friendship has gotten off to a successful start, you have to keep it going.
Ideally over a lifetime. A few very useful tips can make this happen.

If the zest has gone out of the starter, feed it something nice and sweet.
Simply add a bit of sugar or honey to the water when you feed it. Ta da! It's feeling great again! Even better is to work generously with the dough. Sourdough starters are

happiest when they are being used and fed.

Rye flour is the starter's darling.
If the sourdough starter smells so strongly of vinegar that it tickles your nose, rye flour can help. One tablespoon is enough to fire up the lactic acid bacteria and the yeast, which can flex their muscles against too much acetic acid.

The life of a sourdough starter is nearly endless.
I was introduced to robustly bubbling ancient specimens in the Sourdough Library. It's all a matter of care and location. The cold slumber in the refrigerator stops the bubbling and allows the starter to rest until the next bread is baked. Sourdough starters are undemanding; they generally weather hibernation without complaint and often for weeks at a time. Afterwards though, the starter needs your attention. It has to be brought up to room temperature and fed every eight hours: one feeding for every week it was asleep in the refrigerator. Each wake-up feeding follows the 1:1:1 ratio: one part starter, one part water, one part flour.

Hooch means hungry!
When a sourdough starter sits in the refrigerator for months on end, a dark, watery coating forms on the surface. This is the so-called "hooch." The hooch is pretty beastly looking but it really isn't. It only tells you that the starter is very very hungry. The hooch has to be removed or mixed into the dough so that the sourdough can get into shape again at room temperature as described above.

Don't gripe. Get to work!
Sourdough is happiest with this attitude. Expensive kitchen tools aren't necessary. Kitchen scales are helpful as is a food processor but even those aren't a must at the beginning. There are namely fantastic recipes which work completely without the need for electricity. Anything else you might need can be found in every kitchen.

HOW DOES HAPPINESS COME OUT OF THE JAR AND ONTO THE TABLE?

When I first started baking bread, I constantly stumbled over some confusing details.
For example, I had read that different kinds of flour absorb different amounts of water. Did I have to vary the amount of water when I substituted spelt flour for wheat flour in a recipe? I researched this and fell into a mass of information. Not only are flours different from one another, but the amount of protein is also important and so is whether the flour is finely milled or whole grain. On top of that, the vintage of the flour can play a role, as can the mill where it was ground and the weather conditions under which the grain ripened. American flours generally absorb more water than European flours and it is additionally important whether the flour is fresh or has been stored … I was ready to throw in the kitchen towel. And all I wanted to do was bake good bread and not get a PhD in sourdough.

Expecting too much at once from a sourdough friendship can be frustrating.
Nobody has to fiddle around with scalding and soaked grains from the start or learn the entire spectrum of sourdough vocabulary. Keeping our finger on the slow-down button makes it easier to get involved with sourdough. No foreign words and a lot of fun. Free from complicated dough processes but with good, useful recipes.

It is good advice to have both feet firmly on the kitchen floor when the sourdough adventure begins.
Sentences like: "I'll never be able to do that" are absolutely not allowed. Everyone can do it! Because it's easy if you don't complicate things. When you go after sourdough you get much more than just good bread. Sourdough is happiness in a jar. There's no denying it. The more you bake and experience, the more happiness you feel. Both the baker and the sourdough.

Once the friendship has been strengthened one loaf of sourdough bread at a time, it deepens.
Through books, videos and blogs and Facebook groups* filled with magnificent photos of croissants, bagels and baguettes. Masterpieces in dough which make you want to prostrate yourself in front of them and praise the bakers. Thank you for the respect with which you treat the bread and which shines through your art.

Sourdough starters get better and better the more they experience.
That's Karl De Smedt speaking and I am determined to prove it's true. My sourdough will accompany me on my journey to people who open their kitchens and hearts for me. They will tell me their stories and together we'll prove that sourdough has the stuff to make us happy. Beginners! Sourdough pros! Everybody!

13

"Are we really going on a trip?"

"Yes, really! You in a jar, and me in a car."

"The whole way in a car?"

"Sometimes in a plane."

"If I really puff myself up and look mean, they'll think I'm a bomb at security. Then you'll be in for a surprise!"

"You get a few new bubbles and you turn into Mr. Wise Guy."

"Maybe we'll even land in jail."

"Before we do that I'm taking you to Bavaria. You've got work to do."

"What if I get hungry along the way?"

"You won't get hungry. You are traveling in a cooler."

"What if I get hungry anyway?"

"We're not going to be gone long."

"When I get hungry I get really sour and make a stink."

"But you're already sour."

"I can get even more sour and then good luck trying to find someone to make your bread rise."

"And you can try to stay put in your cooler...!"

"Don't close the jar so tightly. I need space to stretch out and I can't see in here!"

"That was my plan! Take a break—you have lots of work ahead of you!"

PATIENCE

DEEP SLEEP

The first thing you hear is silence.

The first thing you see are massive gates and doors.

The first feeling you have is of safety.

The ancient walls are not threatening.
They wrap the guest in a protective cloak. The walls of Wettenhausen Abbey embrace more than 1000 years of history as well as 1000 years of craftsmanship. Rays of sun flit over the weeds growing in the cracks in the wall of the brewery loading ramp. I let myself be carried back in time and watch as barrels with good Bavarian beer are loaded next to bursting sacks of flour lined up in front of the mill. This is where people brewed, milled and baked.

The agricultural buildings face the abbey courtyard. The paint is peeling off the huge doors and behind them is silence. Farm equipment and machines have fallen into a deep slumber.

"Even as a child I took my mother's cookbooks and baking books with me to bed ...
At first I only looked at the pictures but later, when I could read, the recipes were my bedtime stories," says Stefan Heins. Is it any surprise that he turned into the prince from Sleeping Beauty? The man who awakened the abbey out of its deep sleep?

Stefan Heins is 27 years old and studied at the Technical University in Munich.
He can't imagine living in a city; he loves life in his Swabian village as well as its dialect. He speaks about a *"g'scheites Brot"* (a proper loaf of bread) when he refers to good bread. When Stefan Heins talks about his first experiences with sourdough in cheerful Swabian, he laughs. Infectiously.

17

He baked his first bread at 18.
Why? "Because the baker in our village closed down." Stefan missed the familiar taste and decided to start baking himself. His first bread was a magnificent flop.

"I thought that all you had to do was simply bake to immediately make good bread. One with sourdough."

He got his first sourdough as a present from Baker Böck in the neighboring town. "But you can't use it until tomorrow morning" the baker called after him. Stefan didn't listen to this wise advice and started on his first bread dough as soon as he got home.

"I just added flour and water and salt to the mixture the baker had given me and then I shoved the dough into the oven and—nothing happened!" Stefan returned to the baker who had given him the sourdough. He just grinned and anticipated Stefan's answer when he asked: "How'd it go?"

Stefan reported that the bread was hard and flat. That's no surprise, said the baker, because sourdough needs time. Lots of time!

"I didn't know that," Stefan replied.

"You didn't ask!" came the baker's retort.

In the meantime, the sourdough breads obey Stefan's every word.
He gives them enough time to rise and they plump up with joy. He started baking bread in his mother's oven. At some point an oven was installed in the garden. A wood-burning, secondhand model which hold six loaves. But before you can bake, you have to stir and knead. If you are familiar with the amount of dough which goes into six loaves of bread, you know the importance of muscle power. A kneading machine was purchased. One which could handle large amounts of dough. But professional machines are expensive. A used one would solve that problem. What had worked well for the oven in the garden would surely work for the kneading machine. But it didn't work. There just weren't any affordable machines on the market!

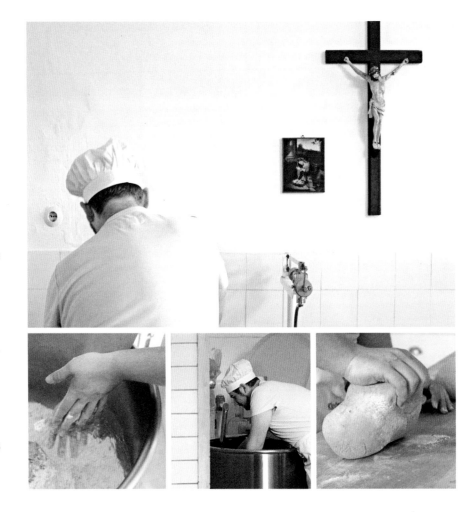

It's a Bavarian custom to open up historic buildings once a year to the public. Everybody should be given the chance to feel the history of a building which is traditionally kept under lock and key. Wettenhausen Abbey also regularly opens its gates on public monument day, and two years ago Stefan Heins was among the group of visitors.* The old abbey bakery is in the basement. A ramp leads the way down to an unremarkable door. Behind it is a small vestibule which opens to the abbey kitchen on the right and the bakery on the left. If you're standing in the abbey courtyard, it might never occur to you to peek through the window at knee level when everything at eye level is so beautiful. But life teaches that even a downward gaze can bring blessings. Stefan Heins turned his attention to the basement window and saw two kneading machines deep in slumber in the old bakery of Wettenhausen Abbey ... Unfortunately the nuns didn't want to sell the machines even though the bakery had long stood empty. Sister Columba, the last baker of the Order, had worked here for many years and everything was supposed to appear as if she had just stepped out the door. The shelves, the table for the dough, the scales and all of the machines ... everything was spic and span and protected against dust with flour-white linen cloths. The bakery of the Dominican Order of Wettenhausen Abbey was a silent memorial to Sister Columba.

A memorial is a good thing, Stefan Heins thought, but it doesn't have to be silent.

He managed, with patience and tenacity, to convince the sisters to let the dough machines in the basement next to the abbey kitchen clatter and rumble again. The huge old oven, which could hold up to 60 (!) loaves of bread, was brought back to life and ever since—thanks to Stefan Heins—there are baking days in the abbey.

I wanted to experience a baking day.

I wanted to watch Stefan's loaves of bread evolve and I wanted to help my sourdough perform its first job. Is there any more dignified place for a premiere than a 1000-year-old abbey?

On top of everything, I had a plan. After my sourdough starter had been freshened up by Karl De Smedt in Belgium and given the okay to travel, I wanted to place our sourdough odyssey under a particularly lucky star. I wanted to take away a blessing.

Twenty loaves of bread were to be baked in the abbey bakery based on Sister Columba's recipe.

Baked with a mixture of rye and wheat flour and sourdough. A lot of sourdough! My little starter would have to puff itself up quite a bit in order to provide enough power for the abbey bread. While everyone was asleep, he performed his first job and did it well. After a wonderfully successful predough, Stefan loaded the kneading machine first thing in the morning. The amount of dough required for 20 loaves of bread is truly enormous.

Impressive, I thought, as I watched Stefan at work.
Everything he does, from weighing the ingredients to kneading and forming the dough, shows that baking bread makes him happy. The way he lined up the 20 loaves of bread, each one separated from the next by a piece of baker's linen, had an element of nurturing. I could have observed him baking for hours. The mildly sour aroma of the dough wafted through the cloister bakery and I leaned against the wall next to the little holy water basin and took in the smell.

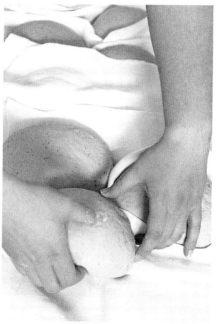

21

**The basin of holy water!
Good heavens!**

I'd lost track of time. Sister Michaela wanted to fill a bottle with holy water for me. She had just been here a minute ago! I ran after her in the direction of the abbey kitchen and caught up with her before she disappeared into the private rooms.

Twenty loaves of bread are ready. Each loaf one kilo of bread personality.

It's nearly impossible to wait until the first slice can be cut. I look at the small jar with the white lid. It's been a long day for my little bubbling friend. He was starving!

I took the large bottle which Sister Michaela had filled up with holy water to Stefan and asked him to feed the sourdough starter for the next stage of the journey. Wheat flour from Wettenhausen Abbey and a portion of holy water prepared him for the trip while fresh crusty bread awaited me.

Sister Amanda came into the bakery.

This was an honor for us because Sister Amanda is the Abbey Prioress. She has taught German her whole life and her laughter bubbles over with pure warmth. She brings along butter. The beekeeper, who is busy in the abbey garden with his bees, contributes a jar of honey. Everybody was been given a slice of bread—the butter melting on the still-warm surface. Because it tastes so incredibly delicious, a second slice with honey follows. "Very good bread!" said Sister Amanda, "Simply good bread!" There's nothing else to add.

klosterwettenhausen.de

WETTENHAUSEN ABBEY BREAD
Sister Columba's recipe

Stefan has taken the trouble to calculate the quantities needed to bake a single loaf—precise down to the last gram! I'm not as fussy as that when it comes to baking. Incidentally, professional bakers really do have to calculate ingredients down to the last gram, so that the bread coming out of the oven always has the same quality. Home bakers don't need to be quite so accurate. I have simply rounded the quantities he gave me.

First make the sourdough:
170 g rye flour
10 g sourdough starter
130 g water
Let the predough mature overnight. Preferably for 16 hours at room temperature.

The next day you should make the main dough:
190 g rye flour
350 g wheat flour
15 g salt
8 g yeast … I'll explain on page 114 why I call the yeast "water wings yeast."
320 g water
4 g bread spices, if desired

Put the sourdough and the main dough into the mixing bowl of the food processor and knead it for 10 minutes at low speed. The dough is ready when it is smooth and firm. Cover and leave in the bowl for 20 minutes. Sourdough likes warm temperatures—about 80 °F is perfect.

TIP
Most ovens reach a temperature of exactly 80 °F if you simply turn the light on!

After "proving" for 20 minutes, the dough is formed into a round shape. Use your hands and a dough scraper to form a shape which is rounded on top and flat below. Press the dough together to form the so-called "seam" on the bottom. Place the loaf with the seam underneath in a banneton which is lined with a cloth and floured. Cover with plastic foil and leave to rise for 90–120 minutes. In the meantime, preheat the oven to 500 °F, which is the maximum most kitchen ovens are capable of. Tip the bread out of the banneton, spray with water and prick the surface all over with a fork. Now put the loaf in the oven, either on a baking tray or on a preheated pizza stone. Bread that is baked uncovered like this will need plenty of moisture so you have to be sure that the oven generates sufficient steam. For example, you can place a shallow container filled with water on the floor of the oven. Later I'll give you a few tips on how to achieve this. Reduce the temperature to 400 °F after 10 minutes and bake the bread for 50–60 minutes. An easier way is to bake the bread in a hot casserole. I explain how to do this on page 57.

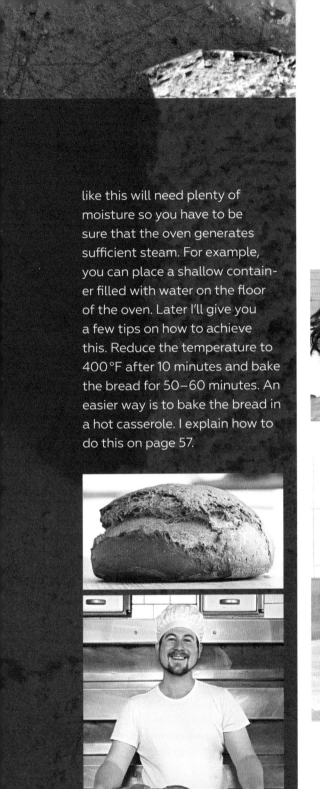

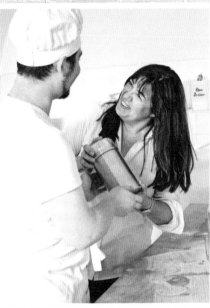

BREAD PUZZLE AND GRAVY

A bread puzzle? I know a giant bread puzzle. Even in 3-D! Ideal for patient people who enjoy a challenge. And the best thing is, you not only solve it yourself, but you can even produce it yourself. 150,000 pieces result in a half wheat/half rye loaf. For those of us lacking the perseverance to create a loaf of bread out of breadcrumbs, there are other ideas of what to do with them. Useful and yummy ideas! In fact, you can make dozens of great things out of stale bread.

In order to avoid cutting yourself, it's helpful to cut the bread into slices or cubes before it turns hard as rock. Slices or cubes become soft when placed on a baking sheet and toasted in the oven. This can be done in an energy conserving way when you use the enormous residual heat of an oven after bread baking. Collect the toasted bread until you have enough to make it worthwhile to turn it into breadcrumbs. Using a food processor is the easiest way, but the old plastic bag and hammer method works as well.

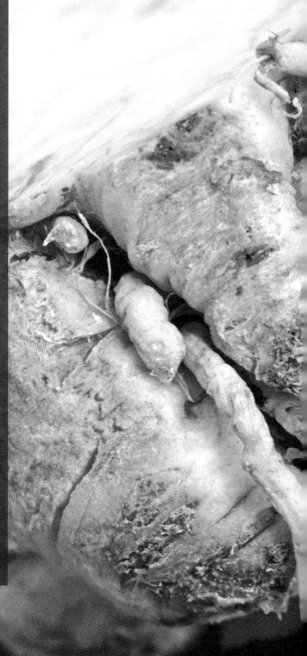

Toasted bread crumbs as a flavor enhancer

The crust of a loaf of bread contains delicious roasting aromas which are intensified by the second session in the oven. If you grind it into fine bread crumbs you can use it as a natural flavor enhancer for your next sourdough loaf. You can replace up to 10 percent of the flour in the recipe for the main dough with bread crumbs. The dough will then need a little more water and a little less salt.

Toasted bread crumbs to coat meat or fish

Pale bread crumbs are a thing of the past. Toasted bread crumbs make the coating into a delicacy.

Toasted bread crumbs as a gravy powder

250 g toasted bread crumbs
100 g instant vegetable stock or bouillon
100 g crisp-roasted onions
50 g dried parsley.

Blend all the ingredients in the food processor until smooth. That's it—delicious! With dried vegetables and more herbs you can make your own individual blend of gravy thickener. Mush-rooms, celeriac, lovage and chives, not to mention dried tomatoes, oregano and carrots are all excellent. You can buy them all dried and ready for use. Drying them yourself is also easy, whether you dry them in the sun, in an automatic drier or in the oven. To make a delicious sauce you just need to add a few spoons of the powder to stock or the roasting juices and then to bring it all to the boil. The sauce powder will keep for months in a jar if stored in a dark, dry place.

PRAISE BE TO CHAMOMILE!

Patience? Not my thing! Even the word is too long.
The weekends are the worst. I want to paint a kitchen cupboard … at the very least! Bake two loaves of whole grain bread … at the very least! Use a face mask, deep-condition my hair, repot three hydrangea plants and meet friends I haven't seen for ages. My weekend lists are sometimes longer than my shopping list on the day before Christmas Eve, and I have never managed to check off all of my "to-dos" by Sunday evening.

Enough is enough! I reach into the bread bag of tricks and bake some patience rolls.
One for breakfast, one for lunch and one to mop up my salad dressing at dinner. Rolls have the advantage in that we can easily take them along in a handbag. I even consider storing one or two patience rolls in the glove compartment. For those certain traffic jam moments.

But how do you turn a tasty roll into a patience roll?
With oats and honey, and don't forget the chamomile! Oats contain large amounts of vitamins B1 and B6. Both are good for our nervous system, and honey makes us relaxed and cheerful because the tryptophane it contains is transformed in our body into the "happiness hormone" serotonin. And last but not least, chamomile has a reputation for making us more patient. And everyone who has ever suffered from stomach cramps knows that chamomile has a relaxing effect.

So how does the chamomile get into the roll?
With an infusion. You can either use it to invigorate the starter or add it to the dough instead of water. A cold infusion is best, because apart from the precious ingredients of the chamomile we also want to retain the nice little microbes which so kindly

bring our sourdough to life. Add a tablespoon of fresh or dried chamomile flowers to a quarter of a liter of water. Leave to stand overnight, drain and dilute with the same quantity of water.

And now, best of all:
Cold herbal infusions can be used to add virtually everything, from money to good fortune, to the dough. Chervil and savory, for example, are supposed to bring wisdom, dill and caraway lead to increased fortune, and lovage, bay and sage to success. Cardamom brings luck, cloves and lemon balm bring love and should you have doubts about the loyalty of your partner, peppermint and rosemary are highly prized. It's worth a try. And if the desired effect is slow in coming, just enjoy the delicious aromas.

PATIENCE ROLLS

The recipe produces a large amount of dough. My impatience is about as large! I like to bake plenty of patience rolls and store them for later because I really like their subtle taste of honey and chamomile! My tip: Freeze some of the rolls immediately! If you just want to try out the effect, halve the quantities in the following recipe.

Predough:
200 g sourdough starter
300 g chamomile infusion
300 g spelt flour

Leave to rise overnight in the refrigerator. Prepare the remaining ingredients the next morning
100 g oat bran
700 g water
100 g honey
4 tbsp runny honey, not hot!
500 g spelt flour
500 g whole grain spelt flour
1–2 tsp salt

Mix the bran with water and leave to stand for a quarter of an hour. Add all the ingredients except the salt and knead slowly in the mixer for 10 minutes. If you think your starter cannot cope with such large quantities, add a piece of yeast the size of a hazelnut. Brush the dough thinly with melted butter to prevent it from drying out and cover the bowl with a damp cloth.
Leave to rise for 4 hours at room temperature. If the room is cool, it will take longer to rise. Tip the dough onto a well-floured board and fold. It will not take long to learn the correct momentum. Once you have got the hang of it, the folding is great fun. Fold the left side into the middle, fold the right side into the middle, fold from the top to the middle and from the bottom to the middle. Turn the dough and start again. And again! And? You got it—again! The dough scraper will help if the dough sticks to the board. After you have folded three times, let the dough rest for half an hour in the bowl. The dough will become more robust with every round of left-right-top-bottom. It is ready when it doesn't stick anymore. To your fingers or the board.

TIP
In the internet you will find plenty of instruction videos about folding. Just google "stretch and fold."

The above quantity of dough is sufficient for 16 pieces. Each piece is formed into a sphere and can be baked in a variety of ways: side by side on a baking sheet or packed in close together in a hot casserole. You'll find a description of the casserole method on page 57. This is the method I find best for the patience rolls because they will turn out particularly fluffy. Of course you can also bake a patience loaf using this recipe … then the patience will come to you slice by slice. The oven, casserole and lid are preheated to 500 °F. The baking time will be 25 minutes with the lid on and then another 25 minutes at 400 °F without the lid.

29

FIDGET FIDGET!
Or: How do you get the dough out of the banneton?

My friend Anne calls people fidgety who impatiently shift from one leg to the other.
When they twist the ends of their hair into skinny cords and chew on their pencil or lower lip. Fidgety is often associated with nervousness but that's wrong. Fidgety is a mixture of impatience and anticipation. A combination of curiosity and eagerness.

You start getting fidgety while baking bread as soon as the rising starts.
The dough needs to relax and recover but we just want to know if and when it'll rise. Particularly impatient bakers should use glass bowls. They allow you a clear view of the dough the entire time and from all sides.

After rising, the dough has to relax in the banneton.
A lot of people find this even harder to take. How will the dough develop? And most importantly, will I be able to remove it from the banneton in one piece without tearing it? Patience, cotton cloths and generous flouring can help here. Durum wheat semolina is very useful in this process. Rice flour works too.

Linen cloths placed in the banneton are wonderful helpers.
They absorb the moisture from the dough and ensure that the loaf develops a kind of outer skin. Heavy handwoven linen is ideal for using in bannetons. But old bed sheets also work.

By the way, the fidgeting could get increasingly worse.
For example, when a specific banneton is used. The ancient wooden basket from a Munich flea market was responsible for double-feature fidgeting. First the gripping question of whether the dough would come out of the banneton in one piece and then the anxiety about whether the inscription "Vienna" would still be readable on the loaf after baking … It was!

TIP
Cotton or linen cloths that are used for baking bread should be washed either with plain water or neutral soap. Never use fabric softener. Unless you like your rustic farmhouse bread to taste of "Caribbean Night" or "Lotus Blossom"!

"What about overtime?"

"What? Overtime?"

"Didn't you count? Twenty loaves of bread! Every single one puffed up by me personally."

"You were really great!"

"Just great?"

"Absolutely unbelievably great. Even the abbey prioress praised you!"

"I actually earned a song or a champagne reception!"

"Hey, you got holy water! I think that's hard to top."

"Something more personal would have been nice!"

"Would getting your own name be personal enough?"

"My own name?"

"Your own name."

"Don't you dare carve anything into me!"

"No, I'm going to write your name with flour!"

"Flour's okay. What kind of flour?"

"Don't be so picky. I'll use wheat flour out of the flour drawer in the abbey bakery."

"Oh, I like that! What are you going to call me?"

"Vitus! From now on your name is Vitus!"

TRUST

A MAN SEES BREAD

A gate made of ancient boards. Rough and clear-cut.

Behind it, ten steps to the right, a man is baking bread.

Good bread! Also clear-cut. Like the man himself.

him good. And I had expected that Vitus would show his best side for Pablo. Sourdoughs can tell when people like them. And Pablo likes sourdough! He likes it so much that he even carried his sourdough with him in a backpack into the Hollywood Hills because he was worried he might otherwise miss his feeding time.

"How should I dress for the photos?" Pablo showed me two T-shirts to choose from.

"And I've also got my best baker's jacket. Should I put that on instead?"

"Put on whatever you feel most comfortable in."

Pablo chose a T-shirt, knee-length trousers and flip-flops.

"This is going to be a disaster."

"Sorry?"

Pablo Puluke walks rapidly to his bakery. I can hardly keep up.

"He really creeps up on you!"

"I hope you're talking about the sourdough?"

"What else would it be?" Pablo asks.

The aroma of freshly baked bread surprises me. Pablo and I had already met the previous day because his recipe includes long periods of rest.

"I wanted to meet your Vitus. He nearly blew the lid off the bread in the loaf pan because he has so much backfiring power."

We had given Vitus a lot to do overnight. He was supposed to make two bowls bubble up, from the bottom to the very top; they each contained an impressive amount of dough. Apparently he had been successful, because Pablo held a fragrant loaf under my nose.

"But we wanted to make the bread together …"

"And we will, but beforehand I wanted to know what your Vitus can do!"

And I came to realize that Vitus can do a lot!

I was proud of my little blubberer, a constant companion on my travels. The care instructions from "Dr. Sourdough," Karl De Smedt, and the holy water from Sister Michaela had clearly done

It was perfectly clear: here was a man in his bakery who was a stranger to artificiality and frills. A man like a loaf of good rye bread: good for you, uncomplicated and his own person.

I would trust Pablo with my family secrets or the PIN numbers for my bank cards. Does that sound risky? Not with a man like Pablo! Someone like Pablo knows that trust is something precious. That explains why sourdough and Pablo get on so well together. They simply trust each other.

"Sourdough changed my life." Coming from Pablo, that is no empty statement. His father was American and his mother was from Bavaria. His parents met on Hawaii, married and then separated again. Pablo's memory of his father consists of not much more than his name: Pablo Puluke Giet. Puluke is Hawaiian for "Bruce." Pablo Puluke's mother raised him alone. He grew up in the part of Fürstenfeldbruck his teachers would later call a "problem district." "You kids are all good for nothing!" was something he heard countless times at school.

Pablo's path was far from straight for a long time.

He had problem friends and was often expelled from school. "I was really horrible. The vacations were so boring because there were no teachers around to tyrannize!"

What followed was the path of a youth who invariably took the wrong turn every time. He dropped out of school, fought with his mother and left home at the age of 16. The first turn in the right direction was when he decided to apprentice as a baker. "I had no choice because I hadn't gotten my high school diploma. Baker or bricklayer." And because Pablo's main goal in life was to emigrate and get rich, he decided that baker was the better choice.

Pablo's favorite flour is rye flour. But it has to be fresh!

"Flour is best when it's freshly milled," he said and laughed out loud when I told him that the German flour packages which list numbers for the types of flour, totally confuse me and I can never remember what they mean.

He told me that during his apprenticeship certification exam he didn't know all the flour types, but he still passed. "And when I did my master's exam I still couldn't list the different types."

"But you probably still passed with flying colors …?"

"Of course! And then I said to the examiner: Look, you don't ever need to know that stuff anyway!"

His path to the master craftsman's exam was anything but straightforward.
Pablo abandoned his first apprenticeship and went to the United States. He took on casual jobs in bakeries and became a successful baker without training. For the first time he felt he was being paid fairly. Unfortunately, he argued with his boss. He told him what no one else dared to say—namely that anything with

more than two legs had no place in a bakery. Pablo was fired. Goodbye company car, goodbye Florida. He moved on and ended up in an organic bakery in Los Angeles. "And the first thing that happened there was that I was put in charge of looking after the sourdough. It was really exciting. It seemed crazy, baking bread with natural stuff like that." Pablo wanted to make sure he didn't make any

mistakes. He took the sourdough starter to his apartment where it lived on his balcony. He was supposed to feed it every twelve hours.
"I was really scared that I might kill it by mistake. I had several alarm clocks to make sure I didn't miss a feeding time, and when I went for a walk in LA, I took the sourdough with me to make sure it didn't die of starvation." He learned to love the sourdough. "Even though at the beginning it was more like a battle. It was exciting to see who would win every day—the sourdough or me."

He soon started to view the sourdough as more than just a fermented raising agent for breadmaking.

Pablo was a man who came from the land of 1000 types of bread and who learned to bake good bread in America. The traditional way. Mostly by hand, with few machines. In LA, Pablo became increasingly fascinated by the breads made from sourdough, good grains and craftsmanship. He contacted his mother and she flew to the US. She took photos of him at the Hollywood Farmers' Market, where his bread was sold on Sundays. She was proud of her son. And things might have continued this way for some time if fate had not given Pablo another little push. In the right direction! But he didn't know that at the time. He injured himself and needed an operation on his arm, although he had no health insurance in the US. He pulled up his roots in LA and flew home to Fürstenfeldbruck. Pablo regained his health and decided to end his dislike of teachers. He trudged on with his training until he passed his master craftsman's exam. "And what do you know? At vocational school all of a sudden I was the one who was sitting in the classroom and saying things like: 'Would you shut up? I want to hear what the guy up front is saying!'"

Pablo says that his life hung in the balance until he was 25.

But there is a good chance that that phase is over now. Now he runs workshops about baking with sourdough and fresh flour, writes recipes which he plans to publish soon, and can be seen on his YouTube channel as "PPG Baker." And he wants to return to the US.

"What will you feed Vitus on the next stage of the journey?"

"I'll grind some fresh rye flour for him. Coarsely. To give him something to chew on. And to give the whole thing a special touch, I'll put on my baker's jacket."

"Very elegant! You can open your first bakery in Hollywood dressed like that."

Pablo laughed and measured the right quantity of water with which to feed Vitus.

"So do real stars actually go shopping at the Hollywood Farmers' Market?"

"Of course they do. The most famous ones are always the first on Sunday morning."

"Does it make you proud to know that great stars have eaten your bread?

"I'm proud of all my bread. No matter who eats it," laughed Pablo, and his eyes laughed too, right up to his hairline.

YouTube: PPG Baker

WHOLE GRAIN BREAD inspired by the Hollywood Farmers' Market

Sourdough starter
350 g whole grain rye flour
350 g warm water 95—105 °F
70 g sourdough starter
Mix all the ingredients thoroughly.
No need for the food processor.
Cover and put on one side.

Predough
240 g whole grain spelt flour
150 g water
14 g salt
Mix all the ingredients thoroughly,
cover with plastic wrap and put
to one side with the sourdough.
Allow both doughs to mature
well! 70—80 °F and 18 hours of
resting time is best.

Main dough
Put both doughs in a bowl.
They will be easy to mix
together. You don't have to
knead the dough and no
machine is necessary. Simply
mix until you have a smooth
mass.
Cover the dough with a cloth
when it is ready and leave to
rest for 1 hour.
During this time, grease a loaf
pan with margarine or butter.
When the dough has rested,
put it into the loaf pan as is.
Flatten the top of the dough
with wet hands, cover the pan

and allow the dough to rest for
a further 1 ½ hours.
30 minutes before the end of
the last resting period, preheat
the oven to 475 °F.
When the 1 ½ hours resting time
are up, spray the dough in the
pan with a little water so that
the surface is damp. Put it
in the oven and bake for 40
minutes!
To test whether the bread is
ready, take the pan out of the
oven and unmold the loaf onto
a rack. If the bread does not
pass the knocking test, put it
back in the hot oven for a
further 5 minutes.

TIP
**The knocking test is a good
way of testing any loaf to see
if it is done. You knock on the
bottom of the loaf with your
index finger as if you were
knocking on the door. If it
sounds hollow like wood, the
bread is perfectly baked!**

FLOUR PATTERNS

Each type of bread has its own natural beauty.
Untamed and pushed into the oven or baked in a casserole. Bread is always lovely.
If you want to make your home-made bread look even nicer, you can use flour to make a pattern on it, or you can carve a design into the dough before you put it in the oven.
Even Pablo, who loves plain recipes, likes to decorate his loaves with his flour signature. When he dusts them with flour and marks them with his sign before pushing them into the oven, his gaze is something like that of parents looking at their child climbing alone into the school bus for the very first time. But maybe Pablo likes putting his "PPG" sign on his loaves so much because his

mother designed the logo for him. Pablo speaks very lovingly about his mother. Sourdough can apparently even heal difficult mother-son relationships.

TIP
It's easy to make a flour pattern. After the dough has rested for the last time, spray the surface with water, position the template and dust the loaf with flour. Remove the template and put the bread in the oven. Easy as that! You can either cut your own template out of cardboard or buy a ready-made one. In large American supermarkets you can find ornaments of all sizes. In Europe you are more likely to find them in do-it-yourself stores. The templates are intended for painters but you can use them on bread too.

41

DIFFICULT TYPES!

There were days when I wanted to throw in the towel. Farewell aroma of freshly-baked rolls; farewell crispy crust …

These obscure types really made my life difficult.

The DIN norm 10355 had eaten away at my fun. It's a profoundly German norm. It divides our flour into types. What a pity I didn't know Pablo at that frustrating time. If I had, I would have called him and he would have reminded me about his master craftsman's exam and told me laughingly:
"Forget it!"
"But I don't dare. Some recipes are full of these type figures."

Wheat flour 405 and 505, and then there's the number 1050, and 812 which is for professional bakers. But 812 and 1050 also apply to spelt, and then there is the spelt flour with the number 630. Rye comes by the number 610 as well as 1150 and 997. But then there's 1370 and 1740 and 1800 as well. And so what is 1800? Right. It's a special type for professionals.

"Have you ever been to the US?"
"Hundreds of times. I love America!"
"Have you ever bought flour there?"
"Yes, I baked a cake for a friend."
"Bread or cake, it doesn't matter. Were there any figures on the bag?"
"No…"
"Any other questions?"

All the figures tell you which part of the grain is in the bag of flour and in which proportion. Professional bakers are thrilled because it helps them to assess the baking qualities of the flour better so that they can always produce bread of the same quality. But does a baking novice like me or someone who just bakes for pleasure need all these figures?

It's much easier to buy flour in the United States.
Here flour is either whole grain or "light." "Light" corresponds to Germany's fully ground flour. And then there is "bread flour." That is comparable to Type 1050. I refused to be intimidated any longer by the so-called "German industrial norm" and have finally gotten to the bottom of these obscure types thanks to a few mnemonics:

The higher the number on the flour packet, the more natural ingredients there are in the flour.
That means more goodness, because the outer layers of the grain contain the largest amounts of minerals and vitamins, so those are to be found in the flour bag with the high type numbers.

Whole grain is always the healthier option.
And whole grain can get along without type numbers. There is whole grain flour which is finely ground but which contains all the healthy substances in the grain. And then there is whole grain bran, which is more coarsely ground.
If you bake with whole grain flour you will be rewarded with more aroma, but you will need to be more generous with the water. Whole grain doughs absorb considerably more liquid.

ALL IS WELL!

Can it be that our memory collects smells?
That the part of our brain in which pleasant memories are stored distributes post-its on which "sense of security," "forever!" and "All is well!" is written?

I felt a magical attraction to a large wooden cupboard.
Spider's webs hung like grey curtains at the attic window and seemed reluctant to let in the sunlight. The cupboard was really old. If you tilted your head to one side and made sure to keep out of the light, you could just detect the tracings of a painting. To this day I believe it showed a bridal couple dancing, but I wouldn't have dared destroy the silvery layer of dust in order to confirm my suspicions.

Next to the cupboard was an ancient mill which performed its duty day after day without complaining.
Beside it stood a large mound of wheat grains. My ritual was always the same: I waded into the hill of wheat and sank into it so deeply that the grains trickled into my little rubber boots. Then I sat down and waited for the mice.

I sometimes had to sit still for a very long time so that the mice would take me for a four-foot-tall member of their own species. Once that had happened they were quite content for me to sit there and watch them.

And what was my nose doing while I sat there?
With every breath it was conveying the aroma of freshly ground grain into that part of my brain in which the post-its are stuck onto our memories. Memories of quiet afternoons in the attic of my aunt's farmhouse. And there they stayed. For decades. Until recently, when I went to visit a mill. I was searching for special flours. Emmer wheat, one-grained wheat, kamut! I entered the room, breathed in and felt my memory starting to search for those yellow adhesive notes. And I saw myself sitting on the mound of grain in front of the farmhouse cupboard, waiting for the mice.

The next day I bought myself a grain mill.
I made room for it beside the toaster and each time the freshly ground flour slides into the bowl, I breathe in deeply. And somewhere between the temporal lobe and the hippocampus in my brain a post-it is brandished on which is written "All is well!"

I'M A MILLER NOW

Part time!

Because it smells so good and is healthy and because I don't have to bother about the type numbers on bags of flour, which I otherwise find so confusing. Grain mills have long ceased to stand for drab design and tasteless breakfast porridge. They have become affordable and are now so small that you can store them just about anywhere.* If you own a food processor it is even easier to acquire your own mill. There are grinding attachments which fit onto all the common brands of processor. Tiny gadgets that work well and use the motor that is already there.**

It's great fun to have your own mill at home.

You can grind the grain fine as powder or coarse and bran-like —you can even grind lentils and peas and use them to make completely new bread creations. Freshly ground flour is healthy and I even find that the bread is more successful. You can feel the difference. Flour from the super-market feels somehow flat and chalk-like, while fresh flour feels "oily" like baby powder when you rub it between your fingers.

On the subject of fingers!

Pointing fingers are banned in my house. Nobody needs to creep out of the supermarket after buying flour there. But fresh flour, organic flour or flour from our favorite miller is simply healthier. Why? Because it contains no additives. Flour from a supermarket has also had the important germ extracted. It is found in the middle of the grain and is oily. In order to make flour fit to store, the germ has to be removed because other-wise the flour would soon go rancid while still in the bag.

Does anyone need proof that fresh flour is particularly good?

Let's just ask the sourdough. How? By feeding one starter with supermarket flour and another one with fresh flour or at least organic flour. The result will convince you. Why? Because the sourdough will blubber away and clearly demonstrate which flour is good for him.

TIP
You can get advice, get to know all the different types of grain and buy good flour for your next loaf of bread or grains to grind yourself. A trip to a mill is also usually a pleasurable break during which you can leave all your cares behind.

45

GOOD WOOD!

One of my favorite types of bread is Paderborn Bread. It's traditional bread from my home region of Westphalia. When I was a child, thick slices spread with butter and apricot jam were a great treat. Paderborn bread is crusty at the top and bottom but soft on the side. The best way to achieve this particular distribution of crispness is to use a wooden baking form.

Baking bread in a wooden form? Absolutely! And does it work? Does it ever! Where can you buy a wooden frame like that? You can make it yourself! It's really worth the effort, because you can bake incredibly delicious white loaves in it—sweet or savoury, or even brioche, not to mention Pablo's Hollywood bread.

I bought a board of wood. Untreated spruce!

Just a finished board of the kind you find on the shelf in any do-it-yourself store. Mine was 4.7 in. wide by 6.5 ft. long and 0.7 in. thick. I also bought 18 wood screws. I had the plank cut to size while I was there:

3 pieces each 9.8 in. in length
2 pieces each 1 ft. in length
2 pieces each 4.8 in. in length

Arrange the pieces of wood correctly.

Screw clamps are useful for this. If you don't have any you will need two extra hands to hold things firmly. Screw the pieces together—and that's it! Or almost it, because before you use the wooden frame for the first time you first have to bake it to season it. Oil it inside and out. I used olive oil but you can also use linseed oil. Rub the oil in well and then bake the form for 30 minutes in a hot oven at 400 °F. Don't panic when it cracks and squeaks a bit in the oven and the kitchen starts to smell like a sawmill. The frame will go darker in the process and will look as if it has been in use for decades.

The baking frame will work with both soft and firm dough.

And this is how: Line a baking sheet with baking paper. Place the wooden frame on it and fill it not more than half full with the dough. Let the dough rise until it has doubled in size and then put it in the oven—two large or four small loaves, tall loaves, flat loaves—depending on how high you fill the frame with dough. You may have to bake the bread for a much longer time than that stated in the recipe, because the bread is insulated on all sides by the frame. But that will make it especially aromatic.

Here's a TIP from Pablo: Butter and margarine separate much better than oil! Oils create a connection with the moist dough and so it will tend to stick more. Butter and margarine on the other hand create a barrier between the dough and the form. And there you are! The bread will slide out of the form when it is done.

"Do you think I could get a part in a Hollywood bread?"

"As the sourdough?"

"No, as the hero!"

"Don't you think that's going too far?"

"Why? I make people happy and I'm good for their health. Isn't that enough to make me a hero?"

"Heroes never have any free time …"

"I don't have any free time as it is. You drive me all over the place and then I have to work."

"Heroes have to risk their lives in the pursuit of doing good deeds …"

"I did that too when we baked our first breads."

"Sounds like the rye has gone to your head."

"Heroes in movies always get the most wonderful women."

"If you stop talking now I'll introduce you to three later."

"Three wonderful women?"

"Exactly!"

"I won't say another word!"

PRIDE

NO "FANCY-SCHMANCY"!

There's a saying that in the evening, when the sky turns fiery red,

"Angels are entering the bakery."

And I'm sure that Frieda is one of them!

Her name was Frieda.

She wore blue-patterned apron dresses, and if you had asked her about her favorite hobbies, she would have said: "Baking and watering the flowers!" Her heart was so big it could fill the two floors of the little house on the outskirts of Nördlingen right to the very top. Full to the brim with kindness and love and the smell of jam, spaetzle and cake! Tray-baked cakes, ring cakes and gâteaux. Sweet and like balsam for the soul.

Frieda lived upstairs. Below her, on the ground floor, lived her daughter with her husband and two daughters. All the doors were always open, which was very practical for the enticing aromas which spread throughout the house. On Saturdays there was always fresh bread. Always! Spicy and with a crispy crust. If any bread was left over, it would go into a baked casserole or bread pudding. Frieda would never have thrown bread away. And although I had never met her, on that Friday, Frieda was with us the whole day.

A business meeting took place on a very hot day in a glass-walled office block.

I was there to meet Johanna Fischer. The meeting was about trends and fashionable lifestyles, and everyone was sweating. Johanna Fischer worked in the purchasing department of a firm which her daughter Delia had founded. Westwing was a company selling good and attractive things for the home—online and with great success. And with an incredible annual turnover of over 200 million euros! We wanted to talk about the kitchen of the future and why quality is cheaper in the long run than low-price bargains. But

instead we spoke about what turns a house into a home and about our children. At some point the conversation became less formal and Johanna told me about her mother, with whom she had baked bread. She spoke about the aroma of bread in the house and that her favorite photos are the ones which show grandmother in the kitchen with her grandchildren.

51

The house in which the bread revival was to take place was the one in which Frieda had done her baking for so many years.
The family still lives here. It's a house built in the early 1950s. White, unassuming, a bit of a labyrinth. The front gardens all around are full of flowers and very tidy.
"Who'd like some coffee?"
"Water?" "Is anyone hungry?"
The Fischers are very welcoming. Guests are embraced and looked after.
"The teaspoons are in the drawer under the coffee machine," called Johanna, "and bring the milk with you, please. It's still in the fridge." It takes less than ten minutes for a visitor to feel at home. "You should take a train with her one day," said Delia. "She talks to anyone and everyone. Immediately. You've hardly sat down and then she starts! When you're with her you're always meeting new people."

"Can you still do it, Johanna?"
I asked. "Can you still bake bread?" "I haven't done it for ages!" I told her about the book I was planning. She raised her eyebrows and smiled. "Do you know how to make sourdough?" "Yes of course, but I would have to look at my recipes, and we ought to ask Delia and Jana whether they would like to join in. They learned all about it from their grandmother."

They couldn't find the original recipe for Frieda's sourdough bread.

But they did unearth her ancient bannetons, her tablecloths and mixing spoons. And the longer they talked about the bread making, the more memories came flooding back. But not the recipe. So we made up a new one.

It was going to be simple bread. Simple and good. With flour from the local fields, so that it tasted of home and something from the garden as well. Elderflower syrup. Homemade! Because Frieda loved to water the flowers. "And when the bread is baking in the oven the whole house is going to smell like Frieda were actually here!" said Delia.

"If she were here, you'd have to wear a headscarf," said her sister Jana teasingly, and with every sentence Frieda seemed to come closer.

There were strict rules on grandmother's baking days. Everyone had to wear a headscarf and an apron too. The flour had to be sieved and you were not allowed to eat the bread until it was completely cold.

"She was very strict about that," as Jana remembered. "Warm bread gives you a stomachache, she said, and no one would have dared to nibble at it secretly."

Westwing is an online retail portal for trendy interior design.

Fashionable furniture, china, bed linen, fragrant candles, cooking pots. Delia Fischer had had the idea to sell high-quality furniture at reasonable prices online back in 2011. On her 27th birthday she gave up her job as editor at the German edition of *Elle* and started her own business. After three months she asked her mother to join her, and shortly after that her sister Jana as well.

In companies like that you might expect to find the managing director wearing shoes that cost more than a lot of people earn in a month. And frequently the long, manicured fingernails of the CEOs might lead you to suspect that the real work was done by the employees with short fingernails. Things are different in the Fischer's company. Here they roll up their sleeves and do the work themselves.

"We were brought up to keep our feet firmly on the ground," said Delia. "That's probably why I prefer simple things to all the 'fancy-schmancy' stuff." Delia Fischer is in her mid-thirties and is responsible within her company for almost 1500 employees worldwide. Mother and grandmother clearly did a good job because she has never lost her down-to-earth approach. "I'd much rather eat a good slice of bread than caviar or anything like that." "Best of all with strawberry jam!" interrupted Jana. "Bread and butter with strawberry jam!" "Let me tell you something," said Delia, "I really can't stand all this talking about low-carb food. I need bread. Every day! And pasta too!"

Johanna baked the spelt-flour bread in a cast-iron casserole.
First of all covered, and then without the lid. The lid was removed so that a nice crust would form and the aroma of bread would fill the entire house. The bread was crisp and golden brown when it came out of the oven, and Jana set the long wooden table in the garden using her grandmother's old china with the gold rim. And when the scent from elder bush on the edge of the garden wafted over, Frieda seemed to be very close. "Do you know something?" asked Delia, "It's sad that the real grandmothers are dying out." And while the others nodded in agreement, the golden yellow butter ran down off the bread and onto the plates …
Sorry, Frieda! Nobody could wait until the bread was cold.

Vitus was given some lemonade for his onward journey.
Lemonade made with elderflower syrup and water, and he was made fit with spelt flour from a little mill in Donauries which grinds the grain from the surrounding fields.

A baking day with three wonderful women came to an end.
And a fourth one was invisible but still among us the whole time: Frieda! The aroma of the bread brought her back to her family. It was a day full of laughter and full of "Do you remember!" and the knowledge that bread making is joie de vivre … and so is eating it!

westwing.de

SPELT BREAD FOR FRIEDA

Predough

200 g sourdough starter
300 g lukewarm water with
5 tbsp elderflower syrup
200 g spelt flour

Dissolve the sourdough starter in the mixture of water and elderflower syrup. Add the flour and stir well. Cover the bowl with a lid or a damp cloth and leave to stand overnight at room temperature.

Continue the next morning with the following ingredients:

30 g kefir
400 g spelt flour
Bread spices
3 tbsp oil
2–3 tsp salt

Thoroughly knead the predough with the kefir and the second portion of spelt flour for 10–15 minutes in the food processor.

If you haven't yet built up sufficient confidence in your sourdough starter you can add a hazelnut-sized piece of "water wings yeast" (page 114) as well. After the dough has been kneaded, add the oil, salt and desired bread spices. Knead the dough for another 3 minutes and leave it to rest again, covered, at room temperature for 1 hour. After the dough has rested, place it on a floured surface. Three sessions of "stretch and fold" with 15 minutes' resting time between each session will result in a nice shiny dough. Put the seam underneath so that the top is smooth and domed when it is ready for the banneton. Cover with a cloth and leave to rise for a further 60 minutes. Bake the bread using the casserole method. 30 minutes at 500 °F with a lid and 30–45 minutes at 400 °F without the lid.

BAKING WITH A SUCCESS GUARANTEE

Cast-iron casseroles are excellent for baking.
But really any casserole will do the job. Tall pots, shallow ones, oval ones, round ones. The main thing is that the lid should fit closely and that there is no plastic anywhere, since that would melt in the oven at the maximum temperature.

Why is baking with a casserole so successful?
Bread loses a lot of its moisture during the baking process. Loaves that are put into the oven "naked," in other words, uncovered, need steam which you will have to add. The casserole method saves the addition of steam because it keeps the bread moist under the lid during the first baking phase!

How is it done?
Preheat the oven together with the casserole and its lid to 500 °F. The pre-formed dough should be put into the hot casserole. Cover it with the lid and place it in the oven. You don't need to grease the form. Depending on the recipe, the lid is removed about half-way through the baking time. Be careful! It'll be very hot! The heat is then reduced and the bread continues to bake without the lid until a wonderful crust has been formed. So do I have any favorite casseroles? I sure do!

Enamel casseroles are very practical. They are light, they conduct the heat well and they are easy to clean in the dishwasher.*

Cast-iron casseroles, sometimes referred to as as Dutch ovens, are a once-in-a-lifetime purchase. They are fantastic for cooking and baking and with increasing experience they get better and better. I'm not kidding!**

Stainless steel pots are great. I have several small ones. I can get two in my oven side by side. That means I can bake the bread for breakfast and a second loaf to give away at the same time.***

Fireproof glass is a blessing for impatient souls. It enables you to see what is happening inside. I managed to rescue my forms at the last minute from my neighbors' garbage can. I like using them for baking and I'm really pleased that I rescued these true design classics. They came from the legendary Bauhaus and were designed by the great Wilhelm Wagenfeld.

Casseroles in every size and shape are available either at German flea markets or in American thrift shops. You can save a lot of money that way. Assuming you know how to clean these treasures. And how do you do that? I'll tell you later!

NEW USES FOR FLOUR SACKS

I have already raved about old mills in this book.
I let the smell of flour make me happy when I'm there, and I also often find nice things to take home with me. For example, I have long been a great fan of the sacks which were once used to transport the flour. Flour sacks like to be useful. I have plenty of uses for them. What is important is that they are allowed to retain their shape; I would find it sacrilegious to snip around at an aged flour sack that had done its honorable duty. There are, however, lots of jobs which flour sacks can still take on without losing their shape.

Transform flour sacks into cushions.
Wash the sacks in the washing machine. Use color detergent, otherwise the writing on them will fade. Sew in a zipper, fill with stuffing and that's it! The elongated shape of the flour-sack cushions looks especially good on large sofas.

Wonderful laundry bags.
Just take a trouser hanger and a flour sack—and there you are! A laundry bag. Made in seconds and you don't even have to stitch anything. Hang it on a hook on the wall or on your clothes stand.

Note organizer.
If you want to keep track of receipts, prescriptions and birthday cards, you need a pinboard. Flour sacks make marvelous pinboards. Cut styrofoam or soft fiberboard to shape and slide it into the flour sack. Fold over the excess and tack it down on the back—that's it!

Where can you find such treasures?
It is worth asking at a mill whether they have any old flour sacks. Other good sources include flea markets, garage sales and eBay.

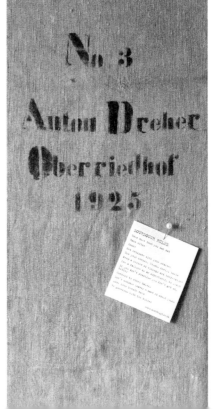

But they don't always have to be old linen sacks …

Smaller bakeries have their flour and grains delivered in robust paper sacks. They can be either white or brown. Some of them are printed with amusing designs, while others are plain and neutral. In any case they are decorative and fairly hard-wearing.

Can you make something eye-catching from old paper sacks?

Yes, you can! I put them to use as wastepaper baskets and assembly points. They provide a very decorative way of organizing rolls of wallpaper and gift wrap, and they also make good umbrella stands. In that case, however, you must surreptitiously insert a bucket because wet umbrellas would make the paper sack go soft.

Ask nicely and you might be given the sacks free of charge.

Bakers like making people happy. They do it every day with their bread, and sometimes they do it with paper sacks as well.

59

YOU'RE ALLOWED TO BE PROUD OF THE FINE BREAD YOU HAVE BAKED!

Fishermen photograph their catch and gardeners their roses. So why not make selfies of our bread in order to preserve our efforts before it gets eaten? Souvenir photos which we can gaze at full of emotion when we have no time for baking. Vitus and I have gazed into the bowls of dough of bakers all over the world. I've eaten bread that has taught me a new way of spelling words like "supreme pleasure." I never tired of watching bakers take hold of their warm bread and beam. It's the look that you usually only see in parents as they gaze at their babies. A radiance which brightens the entire face and that is pumped directly from the depths of the heart into the eyes. For a long time I struggled to think of a word to describe this radiance. When I met Josey Baker from San Francisco I finally realized what it was …
The baker's brilliance!

JOSEY BAKER
Josey Baker Bread
San Francisco / USA
"Sourdough is rigorous science and wild magic."

You could just as well imagine Josey holding a surfboard as a loaf of bread. Josey lives the "Do whatever you like, but do it well dream" of the American West Coast. He baked his first bread seven years ago. "I fell in love with good bread and found it great that people were willing to pay me money for it." Josey started a business. A small shop in San Francisco in which he sells handmade bread. An artisan's bread! He grinds his flour freshly every day and knows the organic farmer personally from whom he buys the grain. Josey Baker makes only simple sourdough bread. Pure, good and only a few kinds. "When you make the bread by hand it gives you energy and then you give your energy back to the bread. It feels as if I were sharing my energy with the people who eat my bread." Josey Baker makes 500 loaves every day. They are offered a slice at a time in San Francisco's top restaurants or sold directly. And because the quantity is so small that not everyone can have some of his bread every day, Josey also writes books in which he shares his recipes.
joseybakerbread.com

MARCUS MARIATHAS
Ace Bakery
Toronto / Canada
"Bread makes everyone happy!"

In the early 1990s war was raging in Sri Lanka. Marcus fled and found a new home in Toronto. He did odd jobs in a tiny bakery and learned how to make good bread. That little bakery is a big one today. They bake bread around the clock. 500,000 fresh loaves every 24 hours. Success like that has many fathers—and in this case also a grandmother: Marcus's grandmother Muthu. "She was a passionate cook and she taught me how to taste what is good." She also advised him to be the best when it came to maths. Two pieces of advice which have proved their worth. Marcus made them into his formula for success: mathematics + passion = perfection in bread making!
acebakery.com

VASILIS & STAVROS EVANGELOU
Apollonion Bakery
Athens / Greece
"Sourdough is the taste of the future out of the past."

If a Greek baker wants his craftsmanship to be passed on, he needs to act as soon as his first child is born. The baker's baby is carried into the bakery, its diapers are removed and its bottom is dusted with flour. Hocus-pocus? In Stavros's case the baptism by flour was successful. At the age of six he baked his first bread; at 26 he was awarded his master craftsman's certificate and he and his father Vasilis have turned the little bakery in Athens into a large bakery in which 20,000 loaves of bread are produced every day. Sourdough bread. Handmade! "It makes no difference whether you make one loaf or a thousand. You have to take the sourdough seriously, otherwise it won't work!"
apollonion-bakery.gr/en_US

TOMMASO RIZZO
Panificio Rizzo
Castelvetrano / Sicily, Italy
"I am a very, very rich man!"

Even as a young boy, Tommaso stood in his father's bakery and played at being a baker. He stirred flour and water together and made his first sourdough without realizing what it was. He has been making loaves of bread for over 50 years. "It's hard work," he says, "but the more you love it, the easier it becomes over the years." He has remained true to his sourdough and still has his old stone oven too. He never wanted to expand his bakery. "Why should I?" he asks, "I'm a very, very rich man as it is. I have three sons and a wonderful wife." And he has time! Precious time in order to pass on the knowledge acquired during his lifetime as a baker. He says he feels grateful when he sees young people beaming with pleasure as he gives them his recipes. Tommaso laughs because he really is a very, very happy man.
panificiorizzo.altervista.org

TOM REES
Pain Plaisir
Bucharest / Romania
"Sourdough has its moods. Just like we do!"

"From the very moment I first came into contact with sourdough, I knew: that is my profession." And Tom Rees learned the profession very thoroughly. He left his homeland, Britain, and went to Paris. He studied the secrets of delicious gâteaux under television and star chefs, and then he discovered sourdough. That took him to good bread and later to Bucharest, where he opened a "French" bakery. Croissants, baguettes, éclairs, everything made with sourdough. Why? Because Tom is never bored when he is baking with sourdough. "For me it's like a friend. A personality. You just have to obey it and find out what it wants!"
facebook.com/PainPlaisir

HAKAN DOGAN
Pasto
Bursu / Turkey
"My sourdoughs are like my children"

When Hakan Dogan laughs, he laughs so loudly that the loaves in the oven shake. He has a powerful zest for life. He describes himself as hyperactive. He bakes 42 sorts of bread every day and writes books on the side for people who like eating. His most recent one received a cookbook prize. Its title is *Ekmeler* or "Bread." Hakan was actually supposed to study medicine. His father, a baker, wanted him to become "something better," but after two semesters in Moscow his son begged him: "Papa, let me be a baker, it's safer for everyone. If I make a mistake as a doctor, somebody will die." He was allowed to return home; he became a real baker and sourdough became his passion. "I would never give away my first two sourdoughs; they're like my children."
obur-dunya.blogspot.de

LETICIA VILCHIS
Masa Madre
Guadalajara / Mexico
"No two loaves are the same. Each loaf of bread is unique."

It started with five loaves per day, and now there are 500. All made by hand and baked with seven different types of sourdough. The bakery is small, but Leticia has big plans. She opened her shop because she loves baking and using her loaves to arouse the feelings which slumber inside us all. "Everyone has memories of bread, memories of childhood. I want people to feel like they did when they felt the bread in their mouth and the crust crunched between their teeth. The way we all felt it when we were children." She bakes Mexican bread and French croissants, and to make sure she is never short of ideas she brings books about baking back to Mexico with her from every country she visits.
masamadre.com.mx

TATIANA IPPOLITOVA
Zelenodolsk / Tatarstan, Russia
"All Russians love the taste of sourdough."

When I met Tatiana she had some "chak-chak" with her. It's a pastry I had never seen before. I admit I had never heard of a region called Tatarstan before either. The former is deep-fried wheat-flour dough with plenty of honey, and the latter is a republic in the depths of eastern Russia. Tatiana is a baker, but at the moment she can be found more often in the laboratory than in the bakery. She is experimenting to produce recipes for bread which will taste just as good when they leave the baking line of the large-scale bakeries in Tatarstan as they did when they emerged from mother's oven at home. "The Russians' favorite bread is dark sourdough bread made with rye," says Tatiana. "We like bread which is very sour and we eat it with oil and egg." If I ever visit Tatarstan I'll try it. I already know "chak-chak."

WOUTER TEMMERMAN
Trainee at Puratos
St. Vith / Belgium
"I always wanted to be a baker."

If I wasn't sick of marriage and Wouter were not far too young for me, I would propose to him. Why? Because then I would have the man who bakes the best waffles in the world all to myself. There is no holding me back when it comes to Belgian french fries, but Wouter's waffles make me forget whatever remnants of common sense I may once have had. Belgian waffles are always delicious, but Wouter makes his with sourdough. Wouter is my waffle hero—and he hasn't finished his training yet. I just can't imagine what he will bake when he is a famous baker. "I never wanted to be anything else, even though my mother said 'you'll have to work terribly hard'," says Wouter. Sometimes it's a good thing when sons don't listen to their mothers.
puratos.de

"Are you also scared of warm bread?"

"Of course not, Vitus. The grandmothers were mistaken."

"How do you know that?"

"Self-experimentation! And besides, I know how to google!"

"Google?"

"That means when you want to find out really quickly whether something is wrong or not."

"Is warm bread wrong?"

"No, but it's been proven that it doesn't cause stomachaches."

"Why did you have to google?" I could have told you that."

"You just make sure that your blubber bubbles don't run out."

"When can I come out of my jar again?"

"Oh, that'll take a while. We're flying to England!"

GENEROSITY

SOURDOUGH CAN BE VERY, VERY STUBBORN

Sometimes the time is ripe for change.

Sometimes you know that but you refuse to listen.

Sometimes sourdough discovers people
and not the other way around.

There isn't any doorbell at the gate but there's a sign warning visitors to beware of the dogs. The gate was dark blue, with a chain to stop it swinging back and forth in the wind. The house stood well back in the garden. The prospect of a pack of Rottweilers made it seem rather risky to enter the property. I decided to whistle instead. I'm pretty good at whistling—especially at whistling loudly. The sound pierced the air. It could clearly be heard in the house, because the dogs started barking. But nobody came out to open the gate.

Barbara, my photographer, and I were waiting in a village an hour's train ride north of London. A boy in a dark blue school uniform rode past on his bicycle; there were green meadows all around; and a red telephone box at the little cross-roads, offering its anachronistic services like an object from another age. The journey was worth it for this sight alone, I thought to myself as I groped in my coat pocket, looking for my mobile phone.

"Vanessa? We're standing in front of your house and are too frightened to open the gate!" "You're here already? Oh dammit! I wanted to get some vegetables. I'll come back right away—I'll be with you in a minute." Soon afterwards a car came to a halt in front of the gate. She leapt out wearing a floor-length black dress, with a basket tucked under her arm and a long blue apron. "I'm confused," she said and led us across the gravel path in the garden to the entrance of her kitchen, "I thought you were going to come later than this."

"We got an earlier train from the airport and sent you a text message straightaway to say that we could be here earlier." She looked at me disbelievingly. "Really?" "Yes, really. You even replied that you were looking forward to it!" Vanessa laughed loudly. "I'm afraid I'm beginning to lose track of all of my messages. I think we'd better start by making ourselves a coffee!"

67

Vanessa Kimbell is a sourdough entrepreneur.

She says: "Sourdough is my soul— as if I could breathe sourdough." She emphasizes the word "breathe" and giggles as she does so. "Does that sound strange to you?"

She reaches for a dish for the predough and searches through a pile of old linen cloths to find the right one before filling a jug with water.

"No, it doesn't," I replied, "sourdough took me by storm too."

Vanessa writes books about sourdough and holds sourdough workshops.

She speaks on BBC Radio about it, researches it, lavishes tender loving care on it and would never choose a holiday destination where she couldn't take her sourdough starter with her.

She is a practising Buddhist, speaks fluent French, has three children, a house and garden and loves pantries filled with homemade goodies and old kitchen utensils. When she talks about sourdough it sounds as if she is talking about a friend. She describes it as "modest and proud at the same time" and calls it her "source of energy."

And when she tells of the stubbornness with which sourdough has fought for its place in her life, I begin to understand the special relationship between them both.

She was nine when she took her first bite of sourdough bread.

In Nadaillac in southern France. On a family holiday with her parents. After a 14-hour journey she was finally allowed to get out of the car. Her gaze fell on a tree. A walnut tree with rough bark. She climbed up and only came back down reluctantly when her parents called her for supper. They went to the village inn. On the table was a basket filled with bread. Each piece had a crust which reminded Vanessa of the bark of the tree she had been sitting in. There was no bread like that in England. She dunked the thick slices in her soup and was happy.

Vanessa's parents bought a vacation home in Nadaillac and every year she looked forward to summer in France and the bread with the thick crust.

The bread in France totally fascinated her.

She wanted to know how it was made. And because bread is baked at night, she climbed out of her bedroom window into the darkness and ran down the road to Hervé in the little bakery. She watched him and made herself useful. Every night during the holidays. She cleaned the bannetons, scoured the baking sheets and swept the tiled floor. She absorbed the smell of the freshly baked bread and stored that aroma deep in her memory. It was a store that would have to last her until the next summer in the South of France. In England there was no sourdough bread. "When I told people at school how Hervé made bread, my friends said, 'That's disgusting, leaving the dough lying around for so long. Doesn't it go moldy?'"

Even then Vanessa knew that the bread would not go moldy if you allowed it more time.

She knew that it became more aromatic, but in those days most people in the UK preferred bread that had a neutral taste. Vanessa finished school in England and wanted to learn to cook. She worked in a restaurant from three o'clock in the afternoon until nine o'clock at night. As for the first half of the day, which was free, the only thing she could think of doing with that was to start studying part-time. Communication Psychology. Now she was working round the clock. At the age of 23, when she had completed two degrees, she was burned out.

She started suffering from rashes over her entire body and overnight it suddenly transpired that she couldn't digest bread. She paid for every crumb she swallowed with pain, swelling of her joints and fingers, knees and hips. Headache for days on end. No doctor was able to help her and she started to think that she would have to exclude bread from her diet for the rest of her life.

While Vanessa talked about the South of France, Vitus was silently working away under the linen cloth.

In conjunction with wheat flour and tap water a magnificently bubbling predough was being formed in the little clay bowl. "Your Vitus is strong …" Vanessa nodded in agreement and continued to tell how she applied to a job agency for work as a cook. They told her that at the moment there was nothing suitable available but she could start work as an employment agent. "Okay!" I said, "Where's my desk?" She put one hand on her hip and with the other she pushed the milk for the coffee across the table toward me. I could just imagine the power with which she had stood in that office in those days. "They weren't friendly to me, and I don't like that!"

Although completely without prior knowledge, she quickly became the most successful agent in the office and before long she had set up her own freelance agency. She placed mechanics and heating and ventilation engineers with major firms, achieved revenues of £2 million and was proud that even Rolls Royce phoned her to ask for recommendations for specialist staff. "It would be hard to think of anything further removed from baking bread, wouldn't it?" I said, grinning, and could hardly wait to learn how she managed to get her life back on track for making sourdough bread.

We had been so busy talking that we hadn't noticed that night had fallen.

The predough was ready and the main dough should have long been prepared for the overnight proving. Flour, water, salt. Vanessa didn't need to use scales; she measured the ingredients by instinct. "You'll see tomorrow morning that it's the easiest bread in the world to make. We don't even need a mixer to do the kneading." Vanessa beamed as she covered up the dough and we decide to go to bed as well. We planned to carry on with the bread making—and the talking—first thing in the morning.

The next morning the dogs came to greet us.

They were wagging their tails in a gesture of friendship. There was not a Rottweiler in sight. Vanessa opened the gate. Unusually, she had applied some lipstick. She led us over to the herb garden. "I want to pick some sage," she said. "We'll need it for our bread later on." The dough was waiting under the linen cloth in the kitchen. During the night it had stretched and risen and would soon be transformed into a wonderful loaf of bread.

Vanessa cut the sage leaves into small pieces.

"And now, please tell me how sourdough won you over again." I retrieved my notepad from my bag and looked expectantly at Vanessa. "Something important must have happened otherwise you would still be supplying firms with mechanics."

"The long version or the short one?" she asked as she stirred the sage into the soft butter. "The long one. Our flight leaves this evening at 7:30!"

Vanessa was 27 when she married.

Now earning a princely income, success seemed to accompany her every move. Only bread still seemed to have a mind of its own. Whenever she ate bread,

her body protested. No doctor had an explanation for the problem.

The newlyweds planned their summer holidays. Vanessa wanted to show her husband the village of Nadaillac, where she had so often spent the summer, and of course the bakery to which she had crept every night in order to experience the aroma of freshly baked bread.

On the very first morning she ran over to Hervé's bakery.

He hugged her and gave her a large loaf of fresh bread. Before leaving the shop Vanessa tore a piece of bread from the loaf and chewed it happily. It was still warm. She carried the bread home. It was all quiet in the

vacation cottage. Vanessa put Hervé's bread on the table, cut a thick slice and spread it with butter. Then another slice and yet another. When her husband came down to the kitchen there were only crumbs left on the table. "I must have looked as guilty as a puppy that has chewed somebody's shoe." The fresh bread was irresistible. Vanessa and her husband both waited for the usual sickness. But nothing happened.

"In the following weeks of our vacation I ate nothing but bread. Hervé's bread." Vanessa chuckled happily. "Bread and butter, bread and jam, bread and cheese and still more cheese; bread and honey and bread with pâté."

Bread had taken its central position in Vanessa's life once more.
She made plans about which types of bread she would bake and eat with plenty of butter. But back at home in England she had barely finished swallowing the first slice of bread when everything repeated itself just as before. "I was ill for four days with pain, the same as always."

She thought it must be the English flour, so she had flour sent from France.
No luck. Her body reacted with sickness again. Vanessa refused to give up and recalled everything she had seen as a child in Hervé's bakery—and then she remembered the sourdough. She asked Hervé to send her a jar of sourdough and she began to bake with it. "My first sourdough bread was a disaster," but although it was tough and obstinate, it did not make her ill.
"Do you know what you have in common, you and sourdough?" Vanessa glanced up from the bowl in which she was distributing the sage butter on the dough. "The sourdough doesn't give up until it gets there. Just like you!"

It would be some time before the sourdough reached its goal.
But in the meantime it was quite obvious that Vanessa had big plans. Her first daughter was born. Vanessa carried on successfully providing firms with mechanics, and met the well-to-do ladies from the neighborhood for cream tea and cricket. These well-off, attractive mothers are known in England as "Yummy Mummies." Their conversations alternated between must-have handbags and their children's private schools. "I was one of those 'Yummy Mummies'," said Vanessa, as she wiped her buttery fingers on her apron.

The second child was a boy.
From Monday to Friday Vanessa continued to run her successful job agency, and on the weekends she played with her children. She cooked and baked, made jam and made sure that their home was as cozy as the ones depicted in British lifestyle magazines. When Libiana and William were old enough she sent them to nursery school. A nursery school that was not only private but also very expensive.
At some point the family decided to move to a house in the country and so they informed the genteel headmaster of the genteel private school that the children would soon be leaving the school. The news filtered through and Vanessa made an important discovery: "There was a rumor that we were bankrupt and

taking the children out of the school because we couldn't afford it. Suddenly we found ourselves virtually without friends." She says that she suddenly realized that she had been living an illusion. "I was judged only by the size of my car, yet I longed so much for truth and for the real things in life."

"We need to feed your sourdough again before you fly back home."
I was so immersed in Vanessa's story that I had almost forgotten. I couldn't bear even to think about the bad mood Vitus would be in. We fed him with stone-ground wheat flour from Foster Mill in Cambridgeshire and tap water from Pitsford.

But it would take a trip to Uganda, before Vanessa's sourdough reached its goal.
She was invited to tour a plantation on which they grew vanilla. She met farmers who were fighting for their own survival and that of their children. Vanessa was horrified at the unfairness and returned home furious. And ready to change her life. She started to donate the money that she had previously spent on handbags. She gave up her job in the agency and focused instead on what she calls "real life." Her youngest child, Isobel, was born and she

realized that sourdough was her true vocation.

Vanessa put the fresh sage bread on the table—warm and aromatic.
Vanessa is an excellent baker. But not only does she bake marvelous bread; sourdough has provided her with a new profession. In "Vanessa Kimbell's Sourdough School," she teaches people from all over the world how to handle sourdough, and her books provide her delicious sourdough recipes. These days, the chance of encountering Vanessa with manicured hands and fancy nail varnish is minimal. More likely she'll have traces of sourdough stuck to her fingernails … and that looks very, very attractive.

TIP
Vanessa says that the most important thing about baking with sourdough is to trust your own instincts. "Much of what is written in recipes is not set in stone. Sometimes it works because it's warm, and sometimes the dough refuses to rise because it is too cold. Find your own rhythm and don't give up too soon!"

sourdough.co.uk

73

VANESSA'S BREAD WITH SAGE BUTTER

Predough

80–100 g sourdough starter
50 g organic wheat flour
50 g cold tap water
Mix the starter in a bowl with the water and then stir in the flour. Cover and leave to stand for 7 hours.

Main dough

325 g water
400 g organic wheat flour
100 g organic whole grain wheat flour
12 g salt

As soon as the predough has rested for long enough, mix the predough with the water in a large bowl. Then add the flour and salt and mix well. Cover with a damp cloth and leave to stand in a cool place overnight.

Put 100 g butter and a few sage leaves to to one side until the next morning. The butter should be soft when it is used. If the dough has risen well overnight, paint the top with a layer of butter. Carefully spread butter across the dough in the bowl. Be careful not to press down so that the air bubbles which have formed do not burst. The butter can be unsalted or salted. It is

important, however, that it is soft enough.
For the sage bread, chop 6–7 sage leaves with a pair of scissors and stir them into the butter. Heat a rectangular loaf pan with a lid in the oven to 400 °F. Remove the loaf pan from the oven and place a few sage leaves in the bottom. Then carefully slide the dough with its sage-butter covering into the pan. Put a few more sage leaves on the dough and close with the lid. The butter will sink to the bottom of the hot pan and will "fry" the bread from below. Bake for 30 minutes at 400 °F with the lid on the tin. Depending on how brown you would like the bread, you could also remove the lid and leave it in the oven for a few minutes longer.

TIP

Deep rectangular loaf pans are useful because they prevent the bread from spreading out during baking. However, it's difficult to find such pans with lids. If you have a long cake pan, you could simply place it in a large oval braising dish. Put on the lid and then bake the bread as indicated above!

TREASURES WITH A SERRATED EDGE

My grandmother always used to say: "Anyone who can't cut bread shouldn't get married!" I got married all the same. Twice, in fact! For many years I believed that my marriages were doomed to failure because my slices of bread always turned out tattered and crooked. Until I discovered one day: I was simply using the wrong knife. It's too late to find out whether my marriages would have been happier if I had had the right cutting tools from the very start. But I am the living proof that it's a matter of the right bread knife, and not the fault of the bread cutter.

What must a good bread knife be able to do?
In fact, a bread knife is really a bread saw. That's the secret. Bread shouldn't be squashed; it should be sawn. The magic word is "serrated." Only a serrated edge can deal with crisp crusts without tearing the bread apart.
A man called Franz Güde first had the idea. He searched for a blade for "results with fewer crumbs." He experimented and invented the serrated edge with which most of the world's bread

knives are equipped to this day. I treated myself to the original from Franz Güde's grandchildren. A large and a small knife.*

A good bread knife is not cheap, but it will last you a lifetime.
I like the idea that one day I may be sitting up there on a cloud looking down at my son, who by then will no doubt have his own family. And I shall be pleased to see how he cuts the sandwiches for his children with our old serrated bread knife. Good bread knives are indestructible and people say they simply get better as the years go by. You can even send most top-quality knives back to the factory to have them sharpened again.

TIP
It's worth looking out for bread knives at flea markets. You will often find examples that are in good condition because many people do not know what treasures are to be found in Granny's kitchen drawer.

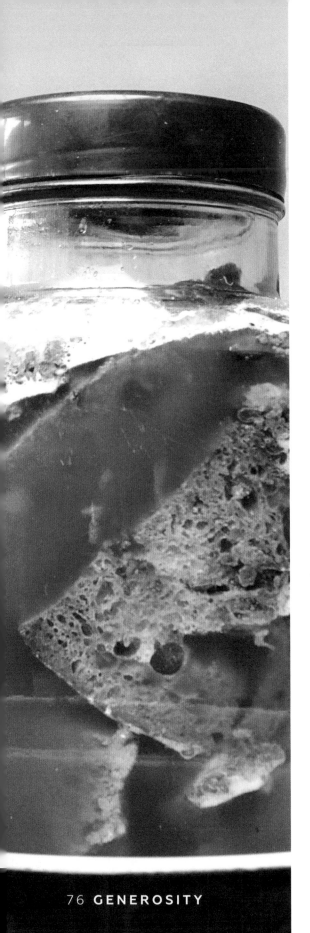

SOURDOUGH AS A BEAUTY TREATMENT

There are sourdough starters that smell of fresh muesli. Fruity ones and creamy ones, strong and weak ones, light and dark ones … but there are never too many.
No leftover sourdough starter should ever be thrown away, because you can use it for many things apart from making bread. It makes us beautiful! Inside and out!

Sourdough sandwich

Rye bread makes us beautiful from the inside! Why? Because rye contains large amounts of B-complex vitamins: B1, B2, B6 and a large amount of folic acid. They all help to beautify our skin and hair. And if you eat the fermented dough with bread and butter, it will also help to strengthen your immune system.

Sourdough mask

Sourdough makes a wonderful face mask. Completely without perfume and chemical ingredients, but highly effective. Why? Because it contains magnesium and zinc as well as those healthy B vitamins. It all helps to keep the skin moist and to calm stressed skin cells. The skin circulation is encouraged and dryness reduced. Dilute the sourdough starter with water until it can be applied easily with a paintbrush. Avoid the area around the eyes. Wash off after 20 minutes using plenty of water.

Sourdough scrub

To make a sourdough scrub, grind some dried starter with a pestle and mortar. I'll explain later how to make dried sourdough (see page 177). Apply to the damp skin with circular movements. The scrub is beneficial for both the face and body and especially helps in the case of skin blemishes. Wash off thoroughly.

And how can we celebrate all this beauty? With sparkling "Sourdough Sekt!"

I gave it that name because it prickles on the tongue like champagne. In Russia it is known as "Kwas" and is made of old sourdough bread. Ready-to-drink Kwas is a healthy probiotic food as a result of all the lactic acid bacteria it contains. It also prompts a good mood because Kwas can develop up to 2% alcohol. There are countless recipes.

A British recipe for Kwas with tea

350 g sourdough bread, as dark as possible
200 g sugar
2.5 liters water

You could also use 400 g syrup instead of sugar. Homemade syrup is best, so that you know what is in it.
Pour it all into a large jar and leave to stand at room temperature. Before long, the first bubbles will start to form. Leave for 24 hours, then filter it through a cloth.
Pour the liquid into clean (!) bottles and store in the refrigerator.

IMPORTANT: Only fill the bottle half-full because the fermentation process will continue and can make the bottles burst. After 24 hours in the refrigerator, fill the half-full bottles with tea. The tea must be cold otherwise it will stop the second fermentation process. Leave the bottles in the refrigerator for a further 24 hours to mature. And the sourdough sekt is ready for drinking!

TIP
It is best not to close the bottles of sourdough sekt too firmly. Screw caps should not be too tight and recloseable ceramic and metal seals should be loosely placed on the opening. The pressure should be checked regularly.
If you are uncertain, you should use plastic bottles. They are less attractive but save you worrying about explosions at the beginning.
The longer the Kwas is left in the refrigerator, the more the acidic and fizzier it will become and the higher the alcohol content.
I prefer to top up the bottles with peppermint tea instead of black tea. It's delicious!

FRIENDSHIP IN A JAR

Living together with sourdough is an adventure.
An adventure which will reward you with a feeling that seems like a friendship.
Some friendships start out magnificently and then break down. Others never really get started, while others develop slowly. Like in real life.

I have experienced starters that didn't make it easy to become friends.
I had one that liked sunlight. When I put it on the table on the terrace it puffed itself up to double the size, but its performance when fulfilling its duties as a bread maker was decidedly mediocre. Another one smelled so sour that I expected a taste fiasco, but the rye bread was magnificent. I had slow sourdough starters and hyperactive ones. And I had one that insisted on being fed punctually.

And then one day you are confronted with the sourdough starter that really suits you.
You have the feeling that he produces his bubbles just for you and lifts the lid of the jar all by himself from time to time just to rise and greet you. That is the start of a wonderful friendship. A friendship in a jar.

Everyone knows that true friendship can only begin if we really open ourselves up.
The most valuable friendships are the ones we have to fight for because the beginning seems difficult.
That was how it was for me and Vitus. I liked him from the start because he smelled so good. But he took things very easy and preferred to stay in his jar rather than make bread rise. Only when we started traveling did he become really active. Or was it as a result of the tips from Dr. Sourdough, Karl De Smedt? Or from Sister Michaela's holy water? It was probably a mixture of all those things and I'm sure he was particularly pleased that I gave him his own name!

Sourdough friendships 2.0.

The internet is full of great websites on which people share their love of sourdough. There are forums and Facebook groups and countless blogs, newsletters and recipe exchanges. It is really worthwhile googling a bit in order to make the acquaintance of sourdough lovers all over the world.

Sourdough friendships in real life.

When I particularly enjoy a loaf of bread, I sometimes ask the baker if I can visit the bakery. So far my request has never been refused and I have never encountered bad-tempered people in the bakery. This is all the more surprising because a baker waylaid at 9 a.m. has usually been working all through the night. Bakers are such nice people! And it happens far too rarely that someone comes into the bakery to say thank you for a fine loaf of bread. Sometimes during these visits I persuade the bakers to give me a portion of their sourdough starter. Vitus may then bubble away in his jar, offended, but I enjoy the variety when I am baking.

I especially enjoy these bakery adventures abroad.

I really only begin to enjoy my holiday when I am able to visit a bakery. France? Sweden? USA? Wonderful! It takes a bit of initial courage to ask, but by the second and third time you will find it much easier. And even if your knowledge of the language is not sufficient for a conversation … everyone understands the beaming "Mmmhhh!" as you bite into the ciabatta and the sparkling eyes when the bagel encounters your taste buds, because that is the international language of bread.

TIP

Sourdough is a wonderful travel souvenir. When your favorite baker in Taormina or Avignon gives you a jar of starter, you can easily dry it out until the end of your journey and take it home with you. You will find the instructions on page 177. Incidentally, I always have a sheet of baking paper in my suitcase for such occasions. The sun will do the rest. And back at home I'll enjoy the bread which tastes of holidays!

GIVE US THIS DAY OUR DAILY BREAD

They always started out flatter at the front than they were at the back.
And depending on whether they came from the beginning or the center of the loaf, they varied considerably in length and breadth. Sometimes I struggled to manage to push the thick slices between the top and bottom row of milk teeth. I can remember one summer when it was easier. That was because my milk teeth were giving way to my permanent teeth and the rows did not meet properly. When I was given a slice of bread, I used a particular technique with which I could master even the thickest of slices: I dug a hole in the middle with my finger and plucked the soft inner part out one mouthful at a time until only a ring of crust remained. When I tore that apart, the result was more or less a snake-like crust which I dangled down in front of my chin while I ate it inch by inch without using my hands.

It is incredible how detailed our memories become when we think of bread.
As soon as we close our eyes we embark on a journey back through time. And no matter how far away the traveler is from his or her childhood days, for most people, the thought of good bread harks back to our childhood.

The thick slices of bread during my childhood came from my Uncle Roman.
We baked the light bread at home, but for dark bread and pretzels we went to the village baker. I often sat on the back seat and hugged the backpacks in which the bread was to be carried home. Plastic bags? Couldn't be further from our thoughts! The linen bags had often seen many years of service. I used to bury my nose in them until we arrived at the baker's. The fabric had absorbed the aroma of fresh bread.

My uncle was an unusually handsome man.
That was evident in the way the shop assistants began to beam while we were still parking the car outside the shop window. We never had to pay anything when we left the bakery with our backpacks full of bread. For many years I believed that this was because all the shop assistants were in love with my uncle. The truth, however, was that my uncle supplied the baker with flour and received part of his payment in bread.

Uncle Roman was a farmer.
He called an early supper "Vesper" and when it was time for the meal, he took the bread, made the sign of the cross above it and pulled the loaf toward him with his left arm. He reached for the bread knife with his right hand and cut off the slices, one after the other, holding the loaf directly in front of his chest. I have never seen anyone cut bread as beautifully as he did. The slices were perfect too. Each one seemed to echo the grace said before the meal: "Give us this day our daily bread!"

"Nobody loves me!"

"Vitus, you're crazy!"

"Hurry hurry! Out of the jar. Hurry hurry! Into the dough. I get no thanks, nothing."

"The word "Hurry" belongs to me. But my heart belongs to you!"

"How come I don't notice it then?"

"Maybe because you're not listening?"

"I'm always sitting alone here in my cooler ..."

"If I had a daintier figure I would join you."

"I hang around in a refrigerator all by my lonesome. In total darkness, because you always turn out the light when you shut the door."

"The light goes out automatically!"

"I'm lonely!!"

"Look, I'll promise you something, Vitus. We'll travel just a little bit more, you'll meet really interesting people and at the end I'll make sure that you're never alone again."

"Would you stir me up a girlfriend then?"

"Better than that!"

"You promise?"

"I promise!"

FOUR YEARS AS A GHOST ARE LONG ENOUGH!

At some point she felt it standing behind her. In silence!

At first it made itself known to her slowly and then it began really pestering her.

Exhaustion sneaks up quietly on strong people.

One day the black rings under her eyes were impossible to ignore.
This is how exhaustion makes its presence known. And Barbara didn't want to see it. She could have covered up the black rings with make-up, but she wasn't vain enough for that, and at some point she didn't even have the strength. She could have asked for help, but who could she turn to? Her colleagues? So that they could gossip about her behind her back? Most people find exhaustion embarrassing and Barbara was no exception.

Nobody had to tell her what was brewing inside her. She was an expert herself.
Maximum performance in minimum time. She was famous for that. Always the very clever daughter of a very clever father. She had never been able to tell him that she had abandoned science. He died before she had summoned up the courage to admit that to him.

The black rings under her eyes are only faintly visible.
She laughs a lot. The signs of exertion are beginning to fade. And as soon as she starts talking about bread, about sourdough and grains, we know that Dr. Caracciolo has arrived. With heart and soul in her tiny bakery in Årsta near Stockholm.

She studied experimental psychology and epidemiology and worked in a hospital in Rome.
She loved her work. But she was one of those people who always do a little more than was really necessary. A little more every day. And that adds up.
She could feel the dark clouds welling up inside her, but she continued to function. A move would help, she thought. The offer from a Swedish university came at just the right moment. She left Rome and moved to Stockholm.
From the Mediterranean sun to the Midnight Sun. From the warm South to the frozen North. At first she couldn't cope with the food and for months she ate nothing but carrots and crispbread. "They were the only things I could eat," she explained while putting on her apron. "I ate so many carrots during that time that at some point my face turned yellow.

85

Barbara Elisi Caracciolo is a woman who always delivers what is required.
Good marks, scientific papers, degrees, and more degrees. "Everyone expected me to be perfect. Successful and perfect. She did what was expected of her and collected a remarkable list of academic titles. A Master of Science in Experimental Psychology, another in Epidemology and a doctorate as well. She was very much the obedient daughter of her father, who was the headmaster of a school and who read the encyclopedia in the evenings to relax. A father who believed that only academic titles would make his daughter happy.

"Things will get a bit noisy now!" said Barbara, "because I'm going to switch the mill on."
She poured in the grain and switched on the machine. She buys her wheat from Bo in Ölandsviete, an hour's drive from Stockholm. And emmer wheat is grown by Francesca in Barbara's home region of Italy, in Apulia. You need good grain to make perfect bread, she says. She uses the word "perfect" frequently. But in her bakery it sounds just right. In contrast to the past when her desire to be perfect meant striving for top achievements.

"Bread is the perfect food"
said Barbara and stirred water and cumin in a small bowl. "Complete and yet simple at the same time." We planned to make some crispbread together. "Viking pizza," as Barbara calls it. "Bread is sacred to me. When I'm baking I have the feeling that I'm working on the most exciting thing in the world." She mixed the flours, added various grains and water and turned on the food processor. It was quite noisy but this did not disturb our conversation in the least. Barbara told me how she had met her husband in Sweden and how her daughter Adina was born. "Then suddenly you are a mother and you take a back seat." She wrinkled her forehead. "Don't get me wrong; I love being a mother, but when the child is small it's never a question of what you want, it's always the child that matters." During the first years Adina was often ill and generally never slept through the night.

Barbara worked at the university during the day and wrote her doctoral thesis during those all-too-short nights. She continued to drive herself on to perform, while suffering all the time from a huge sleep deficit. "You wouldn't have recognized me in those days," she laughs. "I looked like a walking zombie."

The food processor had kneaded the dough.
The little room was once again quiet. Barbara planned to open her bakery a few weeks later. The shop itself was tiny: 430 square feet—scarcely larger than the office in which she had previously written her scientific papers. The counter was made of wood painted white and was almost as long as the shop front windows. There was a refrigerator, a few shelves and a large oven. The sign above the shop read "Spigamadre." Barbara had decided on the name of the "Mother of Grains" a long time ago.

At some point the exhaustion becomes a burn-out.

A big bad burnout. It would have been big enough for two people. "I'd lost my own center in order to please others and now I was paying the price." She wanted to finish her dissertation. The countless footnotes were making her nervous. Barbara kept her eyes on her goal and completed her doctoral thesis. She was terrified of the oral exam, but she managed that too. And then she had finished. A great success. The professors praised her but she was unable to feel pride herself. She carried on and continued to function. She called home in Italy and told her father of her academic success. In the evening, when she returned home, she searched for some form of compensation. She found bread fascinating. She began writing a blog about it. She researched its history and the history of baking.

She approached it like a scientist but she realized that she had had enough of all the theory. She needed to put it into practice. She wanted to smell it, feel it and bite into it. "You can't imagine how much I longed for a life without pressure and without footnotes."

The dough thudded loudly onto the table.

Barbara pulled it out lengthways and folded it. She let it thud back onto the table top and continued folding. This is what transforms the sticky mass into shiny dough. "You could really say that I spent my last years in science as a ghost. I was present in a way, but I was no longer there."

She thumped the dough so hard onto the work surface that the baskets on the opposite shelf jumped.

And she laughed. A warm laugh which gathers in the soul and

then escapes through the mouth. She breathed in and out deeply and showed her delight in every thud she created with the dough. It is a method which is clearly not only good for the dough.

"Slap and fold" is what the bakers call this way of working the dough.

From that day on I decided to call it the Barbara Flip.
You need strength, a firm work surface and a dough scraper. There should be no flour on the work surface because the dough should stick to it so that it can be pulled from the other end. It needs to be thumped down onto the work surface again and again.
The noise in the little shop was deafening. A group of onlookers collected outside the window.

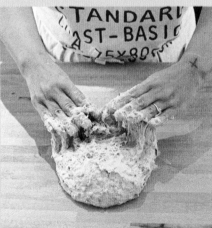

The dough for the "Viking Pizza" needed to rest.
Barbara made some coffee. "I'm afraid it's only instant," she apologized, "the good coffee machine hasn't arrived yet." She told me that her very first bread was soda bread. "I was surprised how easy it was." She became bolder in her baking and tried the next level of difficulty. "If you think that there will always be someone to do the baking in Italian families, you're very much mistaken," she laughed. "I come from an entire baker-less family. My parents were teachers. We bought our bread at the baker's."

Barbara learned how to bake from books and the internet.
Her second type of bread was Italian "filone" bread. It was a success and she found that it tasted like home. She was ready to tackle her third baking project, sourdough bread. Rustic Italian bread like the one they would eat when her family went on excursions to the lakes surrounding Rome. "I hadn't eaten sourdough bread since my childhood. I cut a slice and with every mouthful, precious memories began to whirl through my head." That was the day, she says, on which she fell in love with sourdough.

It was the holiday photos that finally persuaded her to change her life.
"We had taken the photos in Sicily. I looked at the pictures and saw how unhappy I was. Sad and somehow defeated. Yes, that's the right word. On the photos I look defeated." Barbara is not the sort of person who just stands around silently when she is being defeated. She decided to leave the path which other people had decided on for her. She slammed on the brakes and took the next exit.

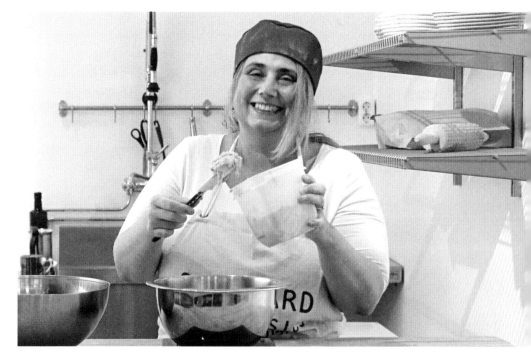

Barbara describes her little shop as a micro-bakery.

She only wants to bake what she can produce herself. Just bread made with the finest ingredients. And she wants to sell freshly ground flour, so that the people of Årsta can taste what good means. Next summer the people will sit in front of the little shop and drink coffee made with the new coffee machine.

Dr. Caracciolo has become "Spigamadre," the "Mother of Grains." Bread instead of books; wheat instead of science. Barbara is happy and looks forward to the future. "And if my father were to look down on my little shop from his cloud, he would be as happy as I am!"

spigamadre.se

It was time to put the finishing touches to the "Viking Pizza."

Now she needed to put plenty of flour on the work surface, so that the crispbread could be rolled out thinly. It is best to use a "kruskavel," a Swedish rolling pin which rolls the attractive patterns onto the crispbread. Barbara looked proudly at every single flat round of dough as it disappeared into the oven.

"I know it sounds strange, but baking with sourdough was the first thing I made just for myself. It was as if I was intoxicated when I discovered how easy it was and how rewarding of your efforts sourdough actually is. I found it easier than anything I had ever done before."

And yet the love affair between Barbara and the sourdough went through the teething stage.

"My first starter did not survive its first week." Things went better with the second one. "I fed her for ten days and she became livelier every day." Barbara sees her starter as a female being. She lives in Barbara's refrigerator at about 40 °F and has continued to make all of her bread rise to this day. What she especially likes about sourdough is its considerate nature. "She forgives me if I feed her too late, if I don't fold the dough perfectly or if I occasionally weigh the ingredients carelessly. She still gives me good bread." Barbara is one of those people who bake by instinct. She loves experimenting freely and trying things out. "You'd better not fly a plane on instinct," she laughs, "but it's fine when you're making bread."

VIKING PIZZA

There are countless recipes for crispbread in Sweden. In the past each family had its own.

This is Barbara's recipe.
150g sourdough starter
250 g rye flour
250 g wheat flour
50 g whole grain rye flour
Some rye flour for rolling out the dough
360 g water
1–2 tsp cumin
100 g mixed grains (sunflower seeds, pumpkin seeds, linseed)
2 tsp salt

Soak the cumin in water and leave to infuse for 10 minutes. Add the "spice water" to the sourdough starter and stir well. Mix the flours in a different bowl.
Mix all the ingredients except the salt together and knead using the food processor for 10 minutes. Cover and leave to rest for 20 minutes. The dough should be slightly sticky. Now add the salt and knead the dough thoroughly by hand on a work surface without extra flour using Barbara's "slap and fold" method. As soon as the dough no longer sticks to your fingers, leave it to rest again.

Put it back in the bowl and leave it to rest at room temperature until it has at least doubled its volume. This can take between 1 ½ and 4 hours.
The dough can also be left to rise overnight—in which case it should be left in the refrigerator.
The best baking method for crispbread is to bake it on a hot stone. But a baking sheet with baking paper will serve as well. Preheat the stone and the oven to 500 °F.
Tip the dough out onto a clean work surface. Do not use any additional flour! Cut it into 16 pieces and form each one into a ball.
Place the balls of dough onto a baking sheet, cover with a cloth and leave to rest again until they have risen once more. Don't be impatient—this can take some time.
Now sprinkle flour on the work surface. One ball of dough at a time should be rolled out very thinly. Sprinkle it with flour as you roll.
The most authentic Swedish crispbread is rolled out using a "kruskavel." If you don't have one, use a normal rolling pin and prick a pattern in each "Viking Pizza" using a fork.

Use a wooden spatula to push the crispbread rounds onto the hot stone. The baking time will be short—only about 4–5 minutes. I recommend keeping an eye on them.
The recipe is also delicious without the grains and spices, and can be made in countless variations.

TIP
Crispbread is ideal as a delicious "emergency ration" in the cupboard. If it is not nibbled at beforehand it will keep for a very long time. It is best stored in a tin, wrapped in baking paper.

BAKING BY INSTINCT

My friend Werner does not have a navigation system in his car. Werner drives intuitively. We recently agreed to meet in a town which neither of us had ever visited before. The train station was to be our meeting place. From there we planned to drive in convoy to a restaurant. The meeting was chaotic. Werner and his car were not there and my mobile phone battery had died. Werner's phone number was buried in my phone and I had only mentioned the name of the restaurant to him once. I was sure that I would never find Werner again. At least, not until I could reach him by phone. I couldn't think of anything better than to drive to the restaurant so that I could at least charge my mobile again. Werner was already there, because Werner drives by instinct.

I can't say the same about myself. I keep losing my way, invariably despite the cheeky grin of my GPS. On the other hand, I'm a pretty good cook. But never according to a recipe. When it comes to cooking I am intuitive.

And what about "intuitive bread making"?
A baker has no need to ask himself that question. His customers want the bread that they enjoyed on Monday to be just as delicious when they buy it again on Saturday. A baker needs precise recipes. Home bakers can be bolder than that! I love baking by instinct.

But it is a question of type.
One person needs a given framework with quantities in order to feel safe. The next one measures the amount of flour by eye and the temperature of the water with his knuckles. So my best advice? A mixture of the two. That applies especially for novices at bread making. As much intuition as possible in order to gain pleasure from the sourdough, and as many weighed-out quantities as necessary to ensure the bread is fluffy and delicious.

I am one of those people who like measuring ingredients using cups.
I find it more pleasurable to pour the flour from a measuring cup than to weigh it out carefully. However, measuring and weighing do have advantages, and for this reason the recipes in this book are noted in metric units. That is the international language of baking. And for those who like using measuring cups there are conversion tables on the internet.*

TIP
Those who don't measure, weigh!
The best method of weighing is to use digital scales. They should be able to weigh at least three kilos and should have a zeroizing function. That will enable you to add the ingredients one at a time without having to use a clean bowl. Digital scales are not expensive and do not take up much space as they are hardly thicker than a slice of bread.

TIP
A little mathematics!
This tip unfortunately functions only in Celsius but it is worth the calculation involved. We need a thermometer that can measure surface temperature, and then we measure three things. First the sourdough, then the temperature of the room in which we are making the dough. Add the two figures together and subtract them from 65. The result will give you the temperature in degrees Celsius for the water which is to be added as listed in the recipe. If you follow this equation the dough will rise like a rocket on New Year's Eve.

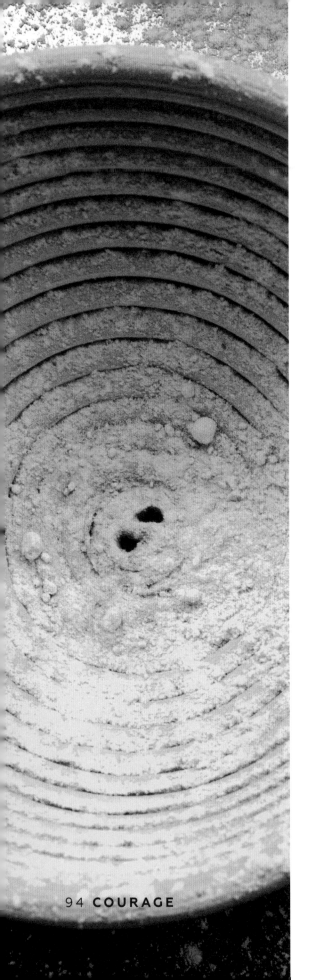

IT'S EASY WHEN YOU KNOW HOW!

I prefer to bake bread with a mixture of intuition and adherence to the recipe.
And I love listening to experienced (amateur) bakers. The tips which I gather from them are worth their weight in gold for a baker like me. Here are a few which I have found particularly helpful. Only the very last one is from me alone. If you follow it you won't need ointment to put on your burns.

Dough rises best in heavy ceramic bowls.
Not only does the dough look attractive, but thick-sided bowls are also ideal for storing useful warmth. Warm the bowl for a few minutes in hot water before adding the dough, then dry the bowl and oil it.

The warmest place in the room is up on top of a cupboard.
Bowls of dough and bannetons like being put up there when the recipe calls for room temperature. Why? Because the warm air rises.

Not fridge temperature!
What applies to cakes also applies to bread. When the recipe calls for eggs, butter or apple sauce it is a good idea to let the ingredients stand at room temperature for one to two hours before use. Sourdough doesn't like having cold feet.

Bannetons must be well floured so that the dough can easily be removed afterwards.
If you line the basket with a linen cloth and flour it lightly you will save yourself the hassle of cleaning it afterwards. The fabric absorbs the moisture and the loaf can be easily removed. You can shake the surplus flour out of the kitchen window.

If you want to enjoy fresh bread you must be prepared to do the washing up.
This is best carried out with cold or at most lukewarm water. Hot water makes the protein in the dough set and then it becomes slimy. A few drops of vinegar in the water will break down the gluten in the remains of the dough and will make it easier to rinse them off.

Shower caps are useful helpers.
A shower cap is perfect for preventing the dough from drying out while it is rising. Of course a damp cloth laid across the bowl will serve the same purpose, but I like to give the plastic cap a second important task to fulfil. Often even a third and fourth task, because I dry out the cap and use it several times.

Stale bread and rock-hard first attempts can be reused.
Not only can you make powder to thicken sauces from them—they will also boost the taste. You can replace up to ten percent of the quantity of flour with old bread. I grind the crusts in the food processor. The roasting aromas give the fresh bread a unique flavor.

Lots of bread types like water after baking.
Loaves of bread without a floury surface will gain an attractive shine if they are sprayed with water after baking. This can best be achieved using a spray bottle as soon as the bread comes out of the oven. The same also applies to loaves which have been baked in a pan. Incidentally, I unmold them 5 to 10 minutes before the end of the baking

time and let them finish off in the oven without the pan. Then onto the rack to cool followed by a gentle shower. For the loaves—not the baker.

Why are hot pans so hot?
Good question! But they are extremely hot! You may just get away with using a tea towel to lift a baking dish out of the oven, but you should revise your plans when it comes to bread. I think it's very important to use thick pot holders when you're baking bread in a pan. Is that a promise? Good!

One more tip as a bonus?
I make my own extra-thick (!) pot holders using scraps of material which I cut into long strips and then crochet together.

A SAUSAGE OF DOUGH FOR ALL ETERNITY!

It takes courage to trust life in advance every day!
To trust that the day is going to be good to us and that the things we do will succeed. I recently found myself looking at a fresh pretzel. It was lying in front of me on my plate and was about to become my breakfast. I put down my knife and traced its curves with my finger. A sausage of dough baked to a golden blond color and wound into a symbol of eternity.

When I thought about the word eternity as a child, I often nearly fainted.
I imagined how everything would go on and on, like a figure eight which never ends. At some point, the room would start spinning around me. I had to quickly think of something else before I ended up lying flat on the floor of my room. Eternity! That is really a very long time. Thinking about eternity no longer makes me dizzy. Maybe my circulation

is more stable these days. I suspect, however, that increasing maturity gives us the courage to look at what might lie ahead. And provides us with the confidence that everything will turn out okay.
Pretzels, for me, have become a symbol of optimism. And sometimes, when I lack courage, I buy a fine Bavarian pretzel and take an eager bite.

Incidentally, I even like the pretzels in New York.

I also like them in Vermont and on the ferry from New London, Connecticut to Long Island. Every time I cross over, I buy one. Pretzels don't only inspire me to philosophical thoughts; they are my favorite in-between snack. It doesn't matter which side of the Atlantic I'm on. American pretzels are different from their Bavarian ancestors. They are not crisp when you bite into them and they are also less salty. The pretzel from the Viktualienmarkt in Munich has coarse grains of salt on it, which most people brush off before eating. That's a custom in Munich. Pretzels in America are soft and mild and taste best when they are warm. And they are always served with mustard. No one can object to that—that's what people do in Bavaria too.

In terms of taste, there is considerable room for improvement of the mustard which is squeezed from a little plastic sachet onto the pretzel in the United States. I therefore consider it my duty as a Bavarian to reveal the recipe for the sweet mustard which is eaten with the pretzel in its home country. The recipe is

over 150 years old. We should thank Johann Conrad Develey, a man who enjoyed experimenting with cooking. In 1845 he acquired a mustard factory and it's not surprising that he started to try out recipes for mustard. He used sugar and vinegar and had the courage to add other ingredients which had never before been found in mustard. And then the sweet mustard from Munich was perfected—and made Johann Conrad immortal

Here is the recipe!
200 g yellow mustard seeds
100 g brown sugar
50 g honey
1 pinch of ground cloves
1 pinch of salt
120 ml wine vinegar
180 ml water

Coarsely grind the mustard seeds in the food processor or by hand with the pestle and mortar. Bring the water to the boil and pour over the mustard powder. Stir and leave to stand for 15 minutes. Caramelize the sugar in a frying pan. Put all the ingredients in a bowl and mix well. Pour into jars and wait for three days. The mustard tastes good immediately but after three days it is truly delicious.

PRETZELS WITH SOURDOUGH AND YEAST

500 g wheat flour
1 packet dried yeast
50 g sourdough starter
5 g sugar
350 g milk, lukewarm
5 g salt
Coarse salt to sprinkle

The sourdough in the recipe doesn't need to be freshly fed. It is added mainly for the aroma, not to make the pretzels rise. Mix the flour with the yeast and sugar. Add the milk, sourdough starter and salt and knead to a smooth dough in the food processor. Cover and leave to rest for 45 minutes.
Knead the dough again briefly and roll into a roll shape about 8 inches in length. Divide into 10 pieces and roll each one again into a roll shape approximately 8 inches long.
Form 10 pretzels; lay on baking paper and leave to rise on a baking sheet in the oven at 125 °F until they have doubled in volume.

TIP
If the work surface is not floured, the rolls of dough will be easier to handle.

TIP
The pretzels will look particularly attractive if they are stacked on sheets of baking paper and frozen for half an hour after they have been allowed to rise. Then they will survive the brine bath without losing shape.

For the brine
1500 ml water
1 heaped tsp salt (10 g)
50 g baking soda

Pour the water into a pan, add salt and bring to the boil. Remove the pan from the stove and gradually add the baking soda (bicarbonate of soda), stirring as you do so. Be careful—it will foam!
Simmer for about ten minutes. Dip the pretzels in the brine one after the other. Take care that it does not spit. Let each pretzel float in the boiling brine for 30 seconds. Remove with a slotted spoon. Put on a baking sheet lined with baking paper and sprinkle with coarse salt. Bake at 350–400 °F for 25–30 minutes.

TIP
If you do not have any baking soda you can use 50 g baking powder instead.

TIP
You don't always have to sprinkle the pretzels with coarse salt. They also taste good with sesame seeds, poppy seeds, pumpkin seeds and cheese.

THINGS ONLY SEEM DIFFICULT AT THE BEGINNING!

Don't give up ... when the sour-dough is sometimes pig-headed and the internet frustrates us with all the photos of magnificent sourdough loaves. The best tip at the beginning is to bake simple recipes without frills and to become a little bolder each time you are successful. When you are learning to read you don't start with Shakespeare, do you?

Don't give up ... when the first and the second—and sometimes even the third—sourdough loaf comes out of the oven as flat as a pancake. It will get better each time. That is my prediction!

Don't give up ... when the first sourdough loaves are an assault on your taste buds. If the first loaf tastes as if it's been soaked in pickle juice, you will need to gain more confidence in handling your sourdough starter. The rule of "more is better" does not apply here. When you have gained more confidence you can rely on the starter to work its magic.

Don't give up ... when the recipes seem to be full of technical terms which you don't understand. At the beginning, many recipes

sound as if they have been written in a foreign language. In this book we try to avoid using technical language as far as possible, but sooner or later you will have to learn the meaning of a few basic terms. You will find the meaning of the technical terms on the internet. There are many good pages. My favorite website is thequestforsourdough.com/lexicon. Here I've always found the answers to each and every question regarding sourdough and bread baking.

Don't give up ... if you feel frustrated at first. Just carry on. It's like the Google algorithm. You order a garden hose in the internet and the next day you'll be bombarded with offers for garden chairs, watering cans and pool equipment. If you really throw yourself into the subject, the right links and the right books will suggest themselves to you.
And the right people too. I'm speaking from experience!

"What's your favorite place?"

"My favorite place is on the coast of Maine and at home!"

"Now you have to ask me: 'Dear Vitus, what is your favorite place?'"

"Dear Vitus, what is your favorite place?"

"My favorite place is in whole grain bread."

"Why's that?"

"Because the grains tickle me when I bubble through the dough."

"Well, do you want me to stir you more often?"

"I've always said it, but you never ask!"

"I thought you didn't want to be disturbed while you were bubbling."

"Even sourdough has needs."

"I know: warmth, flour, water and a couple of yummy microorganisms …"

"Are you making fun of me?"

"I'd never do that! I love you!"

"I love you too!"

"Viiiitus? That sounds like a whole new you!"

"It just bubbled out of me."

"If you could see through your cooler, you'd see me smiling!"

JOY

SOURDOUGH IS THE GLUE OF LIFE

Can you use sourdough to renovate a house? Yes!

Can it transform a life? Yes!

Can it shift well-trodden paths into a new direction? Yes, yes and yes again!!

A man makes tracks.
Tracks into a new life. Happy and best of all barefoot. John van den Broek from Drunen in Holland followed sourdough and a second chance in life. "I'd like to have that every day!" John called out five years ago in his kitchen. He was talking about sourdough bread! John had bought a loaf at the market in Hertogenbosch and was thrilled. He tried to bake bread like that and failed miserably. He had chosen the ingredients well and weighed them out precisely. But bread baking is like life. Even when everything we need is lined up in a perfect row in front of us, sometimes the glue which holds everything together is missing.

John not only learns how to bake but he learns from baking.
When the mixture is correct and you add time and patience, something emerges which is nearly indestructible. In the baking world, that's called autolysis. Quite an ugly word but a terrific gift of nature. Flour, water and sourdough create a net of "glues" which will later help produce a loaf of bread out of the dough. Sourdough also became the "glue" in John's life.

135 million peppers have left the greenhouse since John has worked here.
John has personally helped a large number of them to grow and thrive. Green peppers which have turned red under his care. Something most people don't know: they are all the same kind of pepper. The red ones have been allowed to mature longer. Every day John rolls along the rows of pepper plants. Plucking and binding the plants together. He has traveled more than 3000 miles back and forth along the rows of peppers. He has to stand very still on his trolley. Hours at a time. Row by row. Back and forth.

Six miles a week. Thirty-five weeks in a year. Then the season is over and it's time for a break. The peppers have put their stamp on John. Dark green and ineradicable. Tattooed under his fingernails. "It's always there. On season or off season. The green has blended into my skin and it's going to stay there for the rest of my life," John laughs.

In the past, the free weeks in the cycle of the pepper were used for traveling.
Africa was often the destination. Only in Africa did John really feel that he was living. At this point in time, he was divorced from his wife Sjannie and was living in a house which only felt like a place to sleep between work days. "Sleep, take a shower, eat!" John shakes his head. "Nothing was happening in my life anymore. I wanted change but I didn't know how to achieve it. It was a desperate search but I didn't have any idea what I should be searching for!"

It's hard for John to sit still.
And John can apparently only sit still on the trolley shuttling back and forth along the rows of peppers. He wants everything around him to go well and is thus always in motion.

"Relax, John!" Sjannie says laughingly. She looks at him the way one looks at a puppy who has just stolen a sausage from the table: lovingly and in the knowledge that it's senseless to admonish him because his charm won her over long ago.

In one respect, John has become much calmer.
Ever since there's been sourdough waiting in the fridge for the weekly baking day, John's wanderlust has diminished. These days, baking bread is adventure enough! He can recall exactly how it was when he took his first successful sourdough bread out of the oven. It was April 1, 2013. A lucky day which changed John's life in many ways.

John and Sjannie decide to acquire a new way of thinking.
They took a long trip and on the return flight, for the first time, John was excited about coming home. They made plans to renovate their house. John dreamed of space for the thing which brings him so much happiness and Sjannie also wanted to make more room for herself. She had started taking photographs again and wanted her own studio. An addition was built. Downstairs a bakery for John and upstairs a photo studio for Sjannie.

The extension is so long that John can expend some of his enormous energy with all the steps he has to take.
He prefers to take those steps barefoot. Even when he bakes! Especially when he bakes! He swears that he is at his most creative when he goes barefoot, and it makes him happy that I feel the same way.
"If I have a yearning for red bread, then I experiment with red beets or with carrot juice for orange-colored rolls. I once made green bread with spinach. I wouldn't recommend it." John chuckles about himself and the wrinkles around his eyes twitch with joy.

"What do I love about sourdough?"
John asks himself this question and broods a second before he answers. "I can create life with it." He looks at me and wrinkles his forehead. "That sounds strange, doesn't it? But I'm really talking about something very simple. Mother Nature provides me with the ingredients and I make something living out of it. Water and flour and time and then something alive comes out that makes me happy."

Powerful forces are at work in sourdough.

Something uncharted; enormous. For me it's the "joyous whatchamacallit." It lives between acetic acid and lactic acid bacteria and does its deeds. They can't be dirty deeds because the "joyous whatchamacallit" makes people happy. I'll talk to Vitus about that. He must already be familiar with the "joyous whatchamacallit." For the first time, Vitus is going to have a chance to perform in John's bakery. Of course, John has his own sourdough. The one living in his refrigerator is the one with which he also baked his first bread. He's been well-pampered and fed for years. He's like a house pet to John.

John and Sjannie have built a truly wonderful hobby room onto their house.

In the meantime, sourdough workshops are held here. Small groups; always booked out. Vitus is signed up to produce bread with kamut, an ancient wheat with a particularly hearty taste. My absolute favorite grain.

John bakes ten small loaves which he wraps up and loves to give away as presents. Countless recipes have been developed on the long table in his bakery. Handwritten. On scraps of paper which only John can keep track of. And he's invested in a professional oven. One which manages more loaves of bread than the standard models found in our own kitchens. John's oven doesn't have a large window but only a small peephole. Whenever he puts bread into the oven, he sets the timer for ten minutes. He calls this time "the moment of dancing," in which he forces himself to let his bread dance at 500 °F before permitting himself to look how it has risen.

107

Vitus has given his all in order to lend vitality to John's kamut bread.

And what remains of him in the jar is hungry. We have to pep him up for the next stage of the journey, otherwise he'll turn sour. He receives a strong drink of Dutch tap water and a portion of organic wheat made in a real Dutch windmill. A mill which was founded in 1662. That's where John gets his flours. From Bart, his highly trusted miller. "There is no good bread without good flour," John says. And no strong sourdough starter. Both Vitus and I can confirm that.

Give yourself life and space!

This is John and Sjannie's motto for the future. They have married again. Two people who could not be more different. He prefers to go around barefoot and she loves shoes so much, that she has even hung special pairs on the wall so that she can look at them as often as possible. "Grow the way you like," writes John in Vitus's "passport." Grow and determine alone which direction to take—marvelous advice. Not only for sourdough!

johnzbakery.nl

KAMUT BREAD FROM HOLLAND

Predough

60 g whole grain kamut (Khorasan whole grain, Oriental whole grain) flour
160 g kamut flour
240 g water
60 g sourdough starter

Mix—do not knead—and leave to rest for 8–10 hours at room temperature.

Add to the predough

250 g wheat flour
80 g sourdough starter
10 g sea salt
70 g water

Mix all the ingredients together in a bowl and knead in the food processor for 10–12 minutes. When the dough is smooth and shiny, cover the bowl with a damp cloth or a lid and leave to rest for a further 2 hours. Then form the dough into one large or two small round loaves and lay in the banneton with the seam underneath or—like John—give the dough some support with a cloth. The rising period will take 2½–3 hours, depending on the room temperature. The best way to bake the bread is on a hot stone with additional steam. Bake for 10 minutes in a preheated oven at 475 °F, then reduce the temperature to 425 °F and bake for a further 15–20 minutes. The given baking time applies to two small loaves; a large loaf will take correspondingly longer. The bread is ready when it passes the knocking test.

CHEAT SHEETS AND STEAM

Bread which needs to rise also needs moisture from the outside.
Steam in the first minutes of baking is often important for some recipes. In others, the steam should be distributed equally throughout the entire baking process. Not many of us have ovens like John's, which automatically steams from within. That's why we have to get the steam to envelop our bread and rolls from other sources.

A bowl filled with water is the easiest steaming method.
Simply bake along in the oven. That's all! Steam! Or rather a little bit of steam!

Spray bottles also help in steaming.
Fill the bottle with water (it's better when there hasn't been any cleaning liquid in it beforehand!) and spray the walls of the hot oven or directly onto the bread. And why is hot steam called hot steam? Exactly! Be careful!

John's habit of starting a collection of notes is really good advice.
Not a collection of recipes! A collection of notes like John's is completely analog. Written on analog paper and full of analog ideas. I often print out recipes which I've found in the internet. Or I copy them from books and write my own experiences with them while I'm baking. "Short baking time, kamut instead of spelt, less water or otherwise it will stick ... etc." But also memos after baking like: "Thomas is crazy about it" or "It also works with lentil flour" or "Wonderful for dipping in sauces!" By the way, I'm also a big fan of gluing. I take simple notebooks and cover them with leftover pieces of wallpaper. Then I have my own, highly personal memo baking books. I prefer them all the more with flour dust and butter stains. Totally analog!

If you need a bit more steam, a zeolite stone can help.
Zeolite is a volcanic stone which, by nature, is used to high temperatures. The fact that it can also store water makes it a very useful helper. Place a rough-surfaced zeolite stone plus water in a flat, fireproof form and put it in the oven while the oven is heating up. One part stone to two parts water. Bake the bread as usual. If you want to throttle the steam, simply cover up the bowl. You can find zeolite wherever aquariums are sold or in the internet.

I like the screw method best because it hisses so nicely.
It's fast and works fantastically. You just need a metal pan and screws! Screws? Yes, screws! Nails work too. Everything made of stainless steel. By the way, nails and co. should be untreated. I always run them through the dishwasher before I use them for the first time. You'll also need a plastic syringe from the drug store which holds at least 50 ml, as well as distilled water. This applies only if you are afraid of calcium deposits on the sides of the oven. It doesn't worry me so I just use normal tap water.
Heat the metal pan with its contents up to 500 °F. Put the bread into the hot oven, fill up the syringe with water and spray onto the metal. Quickly shut the oven door. Repeat this procedure as needed or based on the recipe.
And why a syringe? Right! Because the jet from the syringe allows you to keep a distance when water meets the hot metal. Please be careful. Do you promise? Good!

The easiest tip of all is the steamer bell jar.
The only thing you need is a suitable cooking pot and, when possible, a brick. Heat the oven together with the brick in it up to 500 °F, slide in the bread and put the pot upside down over the bread like a glass cheese dome. Remove the pot after 20 minutes and finish baking.

A PUPPY BOX FOR YOUNG SOURDOUGH

Not everyone can tack an entire bakery on to their house.
You really have to envy John. His hobby-baker, free-range enclosure has a lot to offer: a steam oven, shelves for the clear arrangement of an assortment of ingredients, and a warming cabinet for proofing the dough. I have a much smaller space at home for my baking days.

When I bake bread on Saturdays, I first have to clear out the oven.
That's where all kinds of forms and a Dutch oven live from Monday to Friday. There's only room on my countertop for the Kitchen Aid, my food processor and the grain mill. I had to banish the smoothie maker to the cupboard in order to make space for the latter. I guarantee, however, that cultivating sourdough and baking bread is also possible in a small kitchen. We just have to let our good ideas off the chain.

Young sourdough needs attention and especially warmth.
80 °F is optimal. Ovens reach this temperature when the interior light is on. I certainly don't want to keep the light on in my oven for days at a time just to use it as an incubator for my sourdough starter. Besides, in the meantime, I wouldn't know where to store my Dutch oven and co. Professional proofing boxes do exist. They have timers and thermostats but otherwise they just stand around with nothing to do when they aren't needed. My proofing boxes are self-built. Even Vitus grew up in one.

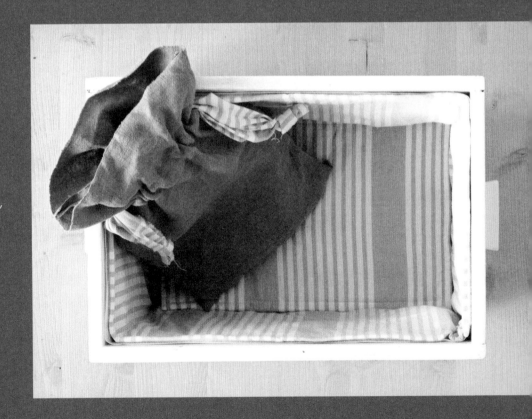

My son calls my proofing boxes "puppy boxes."

I have a round one and a square one. I improvised at the beginning: I would put some pillows in it, a hot-water bottle, sourdough, a second pillow on top, and close the lid! Until my friend Simone came and said: "You can do that much more elegantly!" Simone is namely a professional quilter.

Two cups of coffee later the idea for a chic padded "puppy box" had been born. By the way, Simone has put her instructions on her website. Isn't she wonderful?* The inside padding of the box is easily attached using velcro. This is for a good reason: whenever I'm not cultivating sourdough puppies, the padding goes into the cupboard and the boxes are used as magazine racks or sewing boxes. In case the young sourdough bubbles over out of the jar, the padding can be removed in a second and washed.

How do you keep the puppy boxes warm?

That's very easy! Simone sewed little sacks filled with cherry stones for the round box. The sacks can be heated up in the microwave or the oven and they retain their warmth for a long time.

The other box has a hot-water bottle and soft fleece on the side which both ensure that the box keeps its warmth.

The puppy boxes are not only useful for the cultivation. They can also be helpful for proofing in a bowl. Especially in winter when the room temperature barely reaches 80 °F.

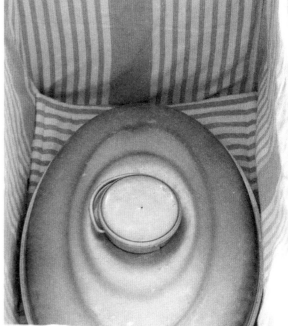

113

WATER WINGS YEAST

Have I already mentioned that my first sourdough bread was a fiasco?
It looked like the lid of cooking pot. Only without the handle but just as flat. I had burdened my young sourdough starter with an impossible task.
From a standing position, he was supposed to puff up a formless bread. The still "unchristened" Vitus was completely overwhelmed.
I took him under my wing the next time. I smuggled a tiny bit of yeast into the main dough. Not enough to insult my Vitus but sufficient to raise the bread. Both Vitus and I were proud of the result.

Since then, I've called this little amount of yeast "water wings yeast."
Why? Because water wings provide lift and security at the same time. Many sourdough recipes work with a bit of yeast. Not even Sister Columba trusted her abbey bread recipe to heavenly assistance and the power of the sourdough alone.

Some recipes in this book call for a bit of yeast.
This is to be interpreted as a "can" and never as a "must." It is totally alright for sourdough beginners to give their starter a helping hand. We become more courageous with every loaf and at some point we can let the air out of the water wings completely.

LOVE LETTERS THROWN IN FOR FREE

Old cookbooks are a treasure.
You might be rewarded for inspecting the kitchen cupboards of aunts and grandmothers. The old printed books are often wonderful just for the cover images alone which feature blissful, smiling housewives at the stove.

The handwritten books are particularly beautiful.
It's a lot of fun to try to decipher the old handwriting and you frequently come upon astounding notes in the margins.

I even found a love letter once. Wedged between recipes for head cheese and chicken in aspic. Such discoveries always fire up wonderful pictures in my imagination. I find old cookbooks at flea markets in Bavaria and in thrift shops in the US.

TIP
When the title contains the word cookbook, usually there is also a baking book inside as well. In the past, recipes for bread and cakes were a part of cookbooks.

And now something good to know when you look through old cookbooks.
In our grandmother's time, yeast was considered something quite classy. Sourdough had fallen out of fashion because it was seen as complicated and time-consuming. Many old recipes thus used yeast as a baking agent. In most of the instructions, however, you can substitute the yeast with sourdough.
As a rule of thumb: one cube of fresh yeast or two packets of dry yeast can be replaced by 200–250 g of active sourdough and the amount of liquid in the yeast recipe is reduced. Some intuition is required, but it's not witchcraft.

And don't forget: Sourdough is treated differently than yeast dough. The key distinction: Folding well is better than flattening by kneading!

"How do your feet feel?"

"Excuse me?"

"I'd really love to know what it's like to run."

"But you do already, you sometimes run over."

"That's true! That was hilarious when I made that huge mess in your kitchen."

"I remember it well."

"If I think about it, I can even walk."

"What?"

"You're always saying 'sourdough starter really takes off at 80 degrees'"!

"Oh, Vitus! Could you please refrain from cracking your corny jokes at our next visit?"

"Let's wait and see! When the acetic acid bubbles through me, I turn into a comedian."

"Please behave yourself! We're baking with children!"

"Okay!"

"Just okay?"

"Sure, okay! I like children!"

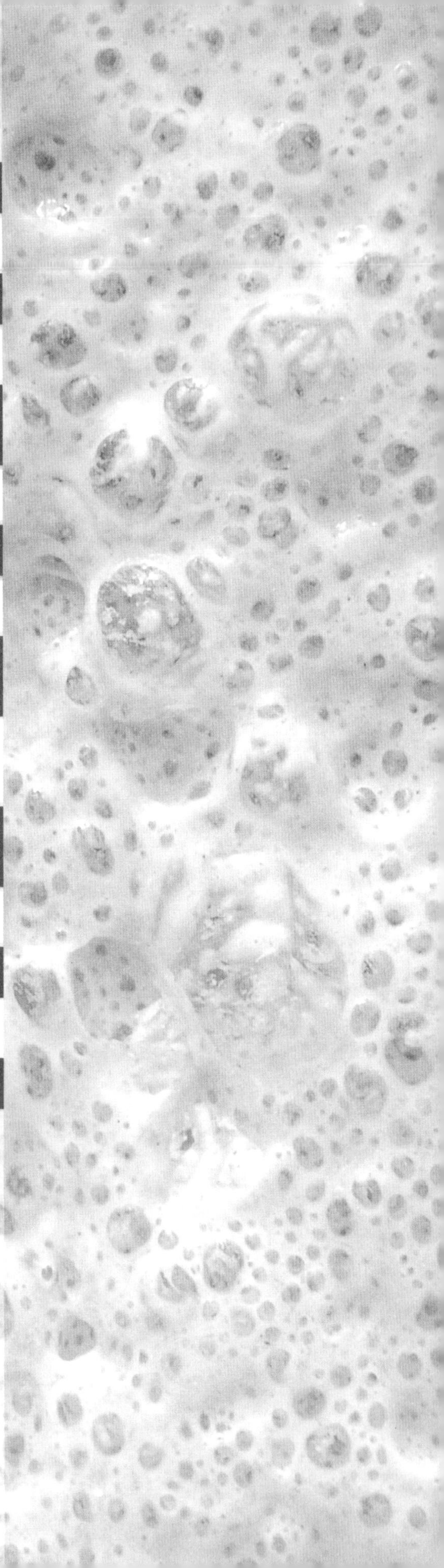

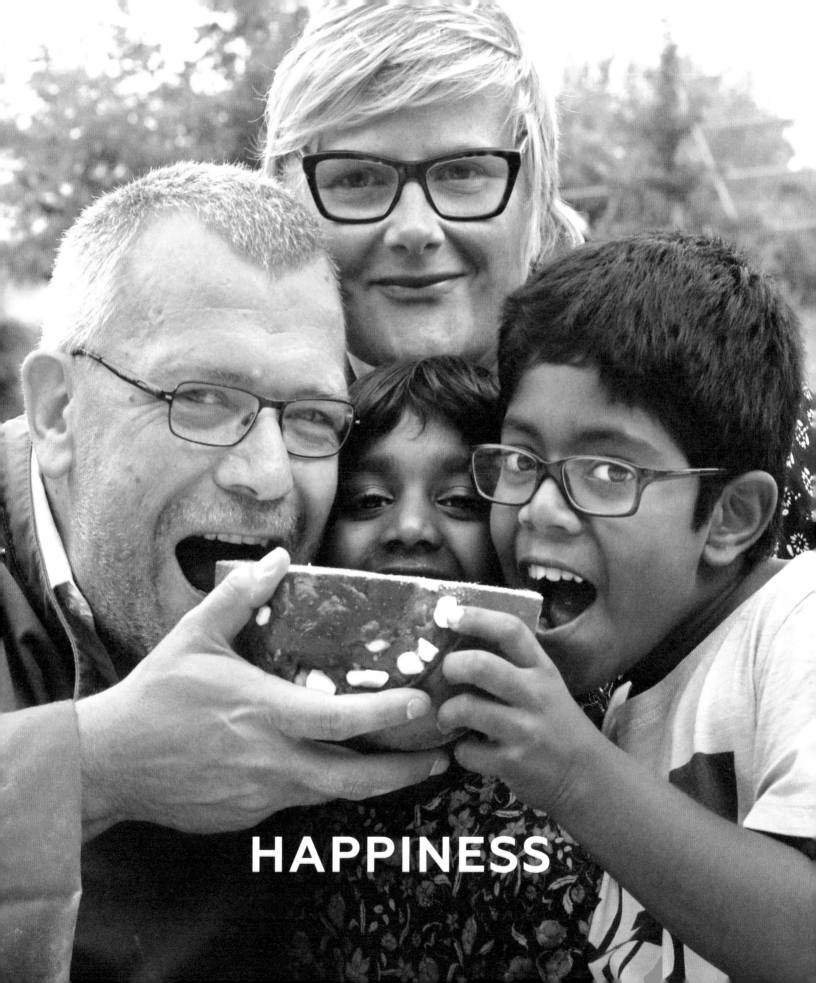

HAPPINESS

LOVE IS THE MOTHER TONGUE

Anil and Lais have a photo album.
Each child has its own.

There are photos of their mothers inside.
Each child has its own. In the album!

Their real mother gives them their
goodnight kiss. This mother they share.

We're all familiar with those moments in which we're in the right place at the right time.
They don't occur very often but when they do, extraordinary things happen. I had just discovered sourdough and was electrified. The oven at home never cooled down because I was so enthralled with the idea that flour, water and patience could turn into delicious bread. I told my friend Susanne of my enthusiasm and my intention to write a new book about sourdough. Susanne introduced me to Stefan Cappelle. One of Europe's top sourdough experts. He became the most important advisor in all of my enquiries. He unlocked the secretive Sourdough Library in St. Vith for me and brought me together with "Dr. Sourdough," Karl De Smedt.
Stefan wants to make sourdough as popular as it once was, and he circles the globe in order to achieve this goal.

"Would you like to see a photo of my children?"
We had been speaking for hours about whole grain flour, bannetons and proofing and were taking a coffee break. What kind of question was that? I definitely wanted to see Stefan's children. He had often spoken of them. About Anil, his son, who could make people laugh and fiddle around with problems until he had solved them. And about his daughter Lais, who had just had a huge party to celebrate her communion and then all of a sudden got very sick. He held his cell phone to show me, and I saw sparkling eyes as dark as bitter chocolate in Lais's deep brown face. Eyes which laughed along when the corners of her mouth turned upward. And Anil, self-confident in his cool glasses. Dark skin like his sister and—in the photograph—just as cheerful.
I had expected blonde Flemish children and the confusion in my face was clear. Whenever Stefan spoke about his wife Katrijn, I had always envisioned a friendly, light-skinned Belgian. "We adopted our children when they were babies," Stefan said and told me the whole story.

119

Women in Sri Lanka who have an unwanted pregnancy are often in great distress.
In order to protect the family, they have to hide themselves. Some cloisters offer these women protection. In one of these cloisters, Anil, and then three years later, Lais, were born. Everything is documented in two photo albums. Even Katrijn's parents traveled to Sri Lanka in order to become grandma and grandpa, and Grandma Maria lent her support to the events from Belgium through texting and prayers. There is a lot of love in the albums. Not only in the way in which Katrijn designed them for her children.

The albums also contain photos of the biological mothers. They are holding the babies in their arms. The pictures document the time before they entrusted their children to others. They are lovely pictures. Pictures of women who have made their decisions with dignity.
The birth mothers chose the parents for their children themselves. Anil's mother was unmarried when her son was born. She described to Stefan and Katrijn what awaited the son of a single mother in Sri Lanka. He wouldn't be allowed to go to school but would be forced to work in order for both of them to survive.

Lais's parents belonged to different castes. Society ostracizes both the relationships as well as the children produced. Lais's mother phoned regularly for a long time after the adoption in order to hear how her daughter was faring. One day the calls abruptly stopped.

When I came to breakfast, Anil and Lais had painted pictures for me.
Mommy-daddy-child pictures. They're happy Belgian children. They attend a small school in a little Flemish town. Both of them have kept the first names chosen for them by their biological mothers. Lais even has two first names: Rangana and Lais. Their parents have turned the shorter name into a nickname. The fact that their darker skin color is different from Stefan and Katrijn's has never been an issue. Only once did Anil say—it was suntan lotion weather in summer—that he would rather be lighter skinned. His pale blond parents answered that they would prefer to be a few shades darker; then they all laughed and the topic was settled.

There is a brick garden building behind the house.

Inside is a stone oven and a mill for the flour. Bread and pizza are baked in the oven and sometimes cake. Everything with sourdough; that is a matter of pride.

To the right of the garden house live the chickens who are fed what is left over after milling and they, in turn, lay the eggs for the cakes.

Today is baking with Daddy day. And with Vitus. The children enjoyed hearing about Vitus's trips and they giggled when I admitted talking with him when we're driving in the car. Anil grinned and winked at me but Lais sort of believed the story. She's still only seven.

The two often bake with their father and always with sourdough, but never with talking sourdough.

And another unusual thing: today we're baking Belgian-Sinhalese style.

Bread is eaten around the entire world. As flat patties and in thick slices. Crispy, or soft and fluffy, spicy or sweet. Belgium and Sri Lanka are very close to each other today on the baking sheet and not thousands of miles apart. We're going to have papadams. Crispy, wafer-thin patties. They're a staple of Indian and Sinhalese cuisine. Classically made of lentil flour, today they're going to be produced out of wheat flour. Papadams are fried in hot oil. That fits wonderfully because Belgium is famous for its fried delicacies. And later, when the patties come out of the oil, they will be sprinkled with sea salt from the Belgian coast and curry from Sri Lanka.

In addition, we're going to have Belgian sugar bread, "Craquelin." Half bread, half cake, baked together with pearls of sugar which crunch blissfully between the teeth with every bite. The dough will be refined with aromatic tea leaves, Ceylon tea, which is not only the national drink but also a piece of Sri Lanka's soul.

The sugar bread not only tastes delicious, but it should also look delicious.

And because it's always eaten up so quickly, several are made at once in reserve. Lais decorates them. With sugar pearls. She concentrates as she works with precision and a sugar pearl disappears into her mouth. Lais looks up immediately at her father and tells him what she did. Lais has diabetes! Everything she eats has to be recorded and balanced out. The time following her diagnosis was scary. She had been at a friend's birthday party and found herself very thirsty. She had soft drinks, many more than usual. She felt wobbly on the way home. A doctor in the hospital diagnosed the danger: type I diabetes! It appears suddenly in children. The immediate diagnosis probably saved Lais's life. Something else probably also saved her life: the magic moment of being "in the right place at the right time," when her birth mother rested her into Katrijn's arms. The illness most likely wouldn't have been discovered in time in Sri Lanka, and then the medications which she needs her whole life would have been too expensive. Her blood count has to be checked day and night and her food adjusted accordingly. A chip in her upper arm discloses the values with the help of a scanner, and she needs several daily injections.

Lais's mother couldn't have chosen better parents for her little girl.
On the day on which Lais landed in the hospital, Lais's biological mother broke her silence. It seems as if she had sensed the danger. She texted Stefan: "How is Rangana?" Katrijn and Stefan went through some awful hours until the doctors gave the all-clear and Stefan could text back: "She's doing fine!"

Stefan Cappelle is a man who doesn't need to use a spoon for baking.
He just scoops some starter out of the jar with his hand and puts it into the bowl. "You can't be afraid of getting your fingers dirty," he laughs, and his son has the same tenacious approach. The papadams are going to be made today with sourdough. That's unusual, but we're baking Belgian-Sinhalese. Everything is done by hand. Papadams are very simple bread patties customarily baked in regions in which food processors are rare. "Not too long," says Stefan. "If the dough is kneaded too much, the patties won't be crispy."

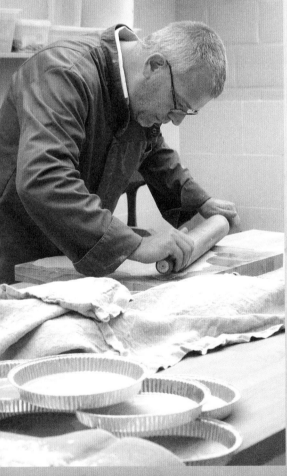

Nobody can teach this man anything about sourdough and bread.

He's not even a trained baker but has always been fascinated with the process of fermentation. When he was as old as Anil, he watched brewing and baking done at home. "Today I prefer to call myself a sourdough brewer and bread lover," he says. And while I watch father and son baking, I can see that the fascination has already infected the next generation. Stefan Cappelle even built the stone baking oven himself. A masterpiece; pure like good sourdough. Created from a few natural materials: sand, lime, bricks and earth dug out of his own garden. The instructions came from the "Museum of Old Techniques" in Grimbergen in Belgium.*

It took four months to build the oven. And then the Cappelles could bake their first loaf of stone-baked bread.

He studied food engineering in Ghent.

His first job after college led him to where he had always wanted to be since childhood: to sourdough. Stefan Cappelle was my marvelous encyclopedia for this book; my sourdough Google. There wasn't one question he couldn't answer. What impressed me still more than his enormous knowledge was his passion for sourdough. Yeast had replaced sourdough in baking. Too complicated, too unpredictable; too time-intensive, many bakers said. "Bakers in large bakeries can't just sit next to the sourdough and wait to see if the dough has risen. However, it must be possible to bake large amounts of good sourdough bread," Stefan says.

How convenient that our Belgian-Sinhalese papadam dough needs to take a break right now. It's resting on the counter. Anil is examining the Polaroid camera with which I photograph Vitus at the end of every trip. Lais wants to feed the chickens and Stefan explains his mission. Stefan wants to introduce sourdough back into every bakery. "Sourdough is in the process of becoming fancy again," Stefan laughs and is delighted that the role he plays here is significant. He runs his own sourdough department at Puratos. A Belgian company which has quietly developed into a highly successful global player. Puratos produces everything needed by bakers and pastry chefs around the world, even Belgian chocolate.

The Sourdough Library, in which treasured sourdough knowledge from around the globe resides in refrigerators, also belongs to Puratos. And the beautiful "Maison du Levain" in St. Vith as well. "The Sourdough House" is a building in which everything about the history of bread baking can be marveled at. In the factory in Groot Bijgaaden near Brussels, experiments are carried out on sourdough to make it possible to produce good, healthy bread in very large amounts. "Even when we transport our sourdough starter in huge canisters, it still has a soul. Sourdough is not a lifeless product which you can simply pull off the shelf," says Stefan Cappelle, and his eyes sparkle with delight.

The papadams have been fried and the Craquelin are baking in the stone oven.
Vitus has to be brought into shape for his next journey before we can try our multi-cultural baked goods. Vitus is fed with a mixture of Belgian wheat and barley flour. Freshly milled and rounded off with a cup of Sri Lankan tea. Vitus has never smelled finer.

The children are hungry.
Lais wants to eat the sugar bread like we all do. A small scales accompanies her meals. At each meal, food is weighed and calculations are made to determine when the next injection is due. Lais no longer cries with each shot. Her parents have helped her to accept the injections for what they are: a new component in her life.

The sugar bread is finally sliced.
It's still warm inside. There are many tiny dark flecks inside. Tea flecks embedded in the sweet dough next to the white sugar pearls. I can't think of a more beautiful image for this wonderful family.
Anil is now ten. His parents have promised that they will all travel together to Sri Lanka when he turns twelve. By then, the children will be able to speak a bit of English in addition to Flemish and French. And when they are adults, they will be able to communicate across the globe because their mother tongue will be understood everywhere. Their mother tongue is love.

CRAQUELIN WITH SUGAR PEARLS FROM BELGIUM AND TEA FROM SRI LANKA

500 g wheat flour
8 g salt
60 g sugar
80 g sourdough starter
15 g yeast (optional)
2 eggs
150 g water

240 g sugar pearls or, as a substitute, cranberries or raisins
125 g butter
5 g Ceylon tea
1 egg to brush the surface
50 g butter for the sugar pearls

Knead all the ingredients except the sugar pearls, butter and tea using the food processor until a fine, smooth dough has been formed. Add the butter in small pieces and continue to knead until it has been worked evenly into the dough. Form the dough into a round ball, cover with a cloth and leave to rest on the work surface. After 1 hour cut off three pieces of dough each weighing 120 grams, form into balls, put on one side and cover again.

Put the rest of the dough back in the bowl of the food processor. Melt 50 g butter, put the sugar pearls in a bowl and pour the butter over.
Mix well, so that the pearls will stay crunchy during baking.
Add the buttered sugar pearls and the loose tea to the dough and knead until everything is well mixed.
Divide this dough into three pieces and form each one into a round shape.
Roll out the balls of dough without the sugar pearls into a circle to make a "plate" of dough that is large enough to cover the balls of sugared dough completely.
Cover the balls of sugared dough with the flat plates of dough and press firmly to form a seam.
Put the balls of dough with the seams underneath into a round, buttered form and leave to rest. This can take up to 4 hours.
Before baking, brush with beaten egg and leave to dry for 10 minutes.
Cut a circle with a sharp knife and fill the crack with sugar pearls. Bake for 35–40 minutes at 350 °F.

BELGIAN PAPADAMS

500 g wheat flour
100 g sourdough starter
200 g water
10 g salt
25 g olive oil for rolling out the dough and for deep-frying.

Mix all the ingredients together by hand until smooth dough is formed.
Form the dough into a ball, cover and leave it to rest on the table. Divide the dough into pieces each weighing 50 g and form each piece into a ball.
Generously oil a work surface and a rolling pin and roll out each ball on this oiled surface until it is paper-thin.
Lay the papadams on a large linen cloth or tea towels and leave to dry. This drying process is important so that the Belgian-Sinhalese wafers will produce crisp bubbles when fried.
Heat some oil in a frying pan and deep-fry the wafers one after the other, either whole or cut into strips.
Grill tongs are a useful tool for turning the papadams. Each side should fry for approximately 10 seconds. Bubbles should form in the process—the more there are, the more delicious the papadams will be.

Do not fry the papadams for too long, otherwise they will taste bitter.
Drain the papadams on kitchen paper and sprinkle with salt and curry powder or other spices whilst they are still hot.
Papadams are delicious on their own or with dips, but they test best of all when they are fresh.

FOOD FOR THE SOUL

… and then it's another of those days, on which the World Wide Web gets on your nerves before the first cup of coffee.
Newsletters lurk in your e-mail inbox to proclaim how over-whelmingly wonderful you are, and Facebook orders you to be happy as soon as you open your account. Mostly in cursive writing on a pastel background or waves or puppies. I should be delighted about the superfood in my muesli, about all of the marvelous people in my life and about my cat. Positive sayings can be a blessing but I prefer to determine for myself where and when and especially how or what makes me happy.

In the past, a bar of chocolate was enough when I was feeling down.
That quickly picked me up again. But if you know chocolate, you also know that the dosage always keeps increasing.
For a long time my nerves could be successfully calmed by handbags. Handbags are lower in calories than chocolate and you can buy them guilt free in XXL. At some point, though, even handbags lost their charm as gratification, even with a set of luggage thrown in for free.

Recently I've been baking crackers!
Why crackers? Because they quickly soothe the soul. Baking distracts from tangled thoughts and, bam! At first the kitchen smells like fresh sourdough and then like fresh crust.
There is a basic recipe for crackers but you don't have to stick to it precisely. The soul feels particularly good when you bake intuitively. I can knead and roll and let a little bit of that excess creativity off its chain.
I use one of the sourdough starters which live in my fridge for the dough. The starter can be cold because it should just make the crackers aromatic, not puff them up. Any kind of flour works. Even a "cuvée" of various types of flour.

Here is the recipe:

100 g flour
100 g whole grain flour
3 tablespoons of olive oil
½ teaspoon salt
150 g sourdough starter
100 g warm water
Fleur de Sel

Mix the sourdough starter with the warm water and let rest for 5 minutes. In the meantime put all of the other ingredients into the mixing bowl of the food processor, add the starter and slowly knead the dough until smooth. According to the type of flour, you might need to add some warm water. Cover the dough and leave to rest for 30 minutes.

Meanwhile, drink a cappuccino or, depending on the time of day, a glass of red wine. Preheat the oven to 400 °F.

Sprinkle flour onto baking paper, lay the dough on top and roll out with the rolling pin until thin. Take a fork and prick the surface of the flat dough at short intervals.

I prefer to bake the flattened dough in one piece and break it apart later. But you can also divide the rolled-out dough into quarters before baking. A pizza cutter works best for this. Brush the dough with olive oil and sprinkle with Fleur de Sel. Bake 20 minutes.

And here comes the best "happy maker" of all.

While the crackers are browning, place a chair in front of the oven, close your eyes and deeply inhale the aroma.

The crackers can best be stored like cookies in tins. But they're usually gobbled up all at once.

TIP

The dough can be sublimely refined with grated parmesan cheese and herbs. Hummus or cream cheese turn the crackers into a great between-meals snack.

HAPPINESS IS ...

... when the bread dough snakes its way out of the banneton and contentedly expands its swollen belly.

When it lands elegantly on to the baking sheet or in the hot pot, and the baker's heart fills in anticipation of the finished loaf, many little endorphins pump through your veins.

But what happens if the dough doesn't want to leave its basket?

If the dough flops onto its side and the little beauty is suddenly full of dents? Luckily we won't have to describe what happens because there is the tried and true paper-strip-lifting method to give a helping hand to lazy loaves.

What you need to do: Cut a strip of baking paper as broad as your banneton and long enough to extend about 8 inches beyond both long ends of the basket. Take a board which is big enough to easily cover up the basket.

When the dough has proofed sufficiently in its basket, the paper strip is laid on top of the basket and the loaf so that the paper sticks out on both the left and the right sides. Place the board on top and turn every-thing over.

The dough will flop down onto the board and it can easily be placed into the pot or onto the sheet with its best side up. Ta da! Happiness!

I have still another happiness helper:

HAPPINESS IS ...

... when the bread, as beautiful as a painting, cools on the grate and perfumes the room with its spicy aroma.

When the crust crackles and the butter can barely wait to melt on the first slice of the warm loaf.

And when you've forgotten the bread until the following day because you were so busy and your eyes just fall shut by themselves!

We luckily don't have to imagine that because good bread can be perked up again even when it's been lying around unpacked all day and night in the kitchen. How! In the bread sauna.

First of all you'll need a plate and a pot. The plate and the hardened bread have to fit into the pot. Cover the bottom of the pot with water; put the plate and the bread into the pot. The bread mustn't come into contact with the water. Put the pot on a stove-top ring and simmer the water until it starts to steam Put the lid on the pot and let the bread sweat. Take out the bread after 10 minutes. It's no longer a hardship case!

WHEN HAPPINESS COULD BE BAKED

Once upon a time, a slice of bread was a gift.
It was the time when happiness could still be baked into bread and making a wish actually helped.
This is the kind of advice you can still find in old books. Rituals which bring happiness into your house and help to prevent misfortune. Who knows? Maybe some of this advice still works today.

At Christmas, bread can perform miracles. Place it for a short time on the threshold of the front door. From then on for an entire year, nothing bad can enter the house.

Pregnant women should place a piece of bread under their pillows. If this is done in the final days of the pregnancy, a gentle and happy birth is guaranteed.

Bread should be broken over newborn babies. The children will develop magnificently.

Bread can help children who don't want to start speaking.
Take a piece of bread, break it and say: "Dear bread break and dear child speak!" The success rate is unknown.

Happiness and bread were inseparable from one another.
But the opposite was just as unavoidable when bread was treated without respect. The result was misfortune for house and home and body and soul. Bad luck was inevitably invited into the house when flour was carried out backwards or a loaf of bread was placed upside down. Swearing in the presence of bread attracted a divine thunderstorm.

An act of sacrilege with respect to bread was an acknowledged sin.
Whoever was guilty of this was almost sure to bring on troubles.
Stolzenburg, a hill castle in the Eifel region of Germany was especially hard hit. According to legend, the castle knights ordered the village baker to bake extra hard bread so that they could organize bowling tournaments. While the knights

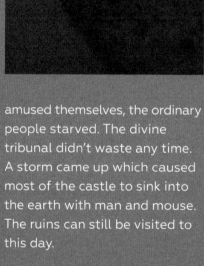

amused themselves, the ordinary people starved. The divine tribunal didn't waste any time. A storm came up which caused most of the castle to sink into the earth with man and mouse. The ruins can still be visited to this day.

Just superstition?
Could be, but in my opinion, there is still an element of truth in these tales: bread should not be taken for granted. It has earned our respect!

HAPPINESS IS NOT JUST FOR LUCKY DUCKS

... even humans strive to be happy.
But it is becoming more difficult to feel this emotion. People are searching the whole world over! Through drumming courses, fasting; vegan cooking classes. On dating platforms, with sugar-free food and tree hugging. Tai Chi, Qigong, Feng Shui and Kombucha.
Every day we are presented with new paths to happiness and the appropriate equipment: yoga mats, pills and fitness clothing, Botox and pilgrimages.
We buy and improve ourselves until we're breathless.

Wouldn't it be wonderful if happiness were everywhere?
Affordable and available everywhere in the world? If we could carry a bag of happiness everywhere we go?

My happiness has many names:
Dinner roll, pretzel, crispbread, baguette, focaccia, bagel and pumpernickel. Sweet or salty, self-baked or purchased at the baker around the corner.

The connection between humans and bread is strong.
When we're on a trip and get homesick for our breakfast rolls, it's then at the latest that we realize the beating of our heart is connected to bread.
Mom's packed lunch with extra cheese, sandwiches in front of the television, a slice of what we call 'Hefezopf', a kind of challah bread, dunked in cocoa, whole grain bread with honey for breakfast. That's what home feels like.

Bread is happiness! In slices and loaves!

HAPPINESS CAN BE CUT INTO SLICES

There are days which feel normal.
They have a beginning, middle and end! You only notice later that it wasn't just a normal day. It was a slice from the meaning of life. A day with moments which are capable of opening your soul. Special moments are not very loud.
They don't call attention to themselves but we would benefit from noticing them and letting them shine within us forever.

"Do you want to have breakfast, Mom?"
He takes off his shoes and hangs his jacket on the hook in the hall. He sticks his nose in the air, sniffs and grins at me.

"Do you want to have breakfast, Mom?"
It was just yesterday that Bob the Builder was his hero and now he towers over me by almost a foot. A foot is a lot if you know that he still collects Pokemon cards and is saving up for his first fishing rod. He started going to parties which ended late. Over time, more parties followed which ended even later. I was often still awake when he came home. It was hard for me to not be able to protect him anymore. I liked to stay awake until he was safe at home. "Tea?" I would ask. Tea seemed fitting on such nights. We would often sit around the kitchen table for a few minutes and drink hot tea.

At some point around then I discovered bread baking.
Best of all, on the weekend and with all of its proofing and resting phases during the day, evenings were exactly the right time to take the loaf out of its basket and to slide it into the oven. Afterwards the finished breads would cool down on the grate and give off their intoxicating aromas. A nocturnal aroma which pervaded the entire house.
Bread perfume was what my son smelled when he came home. He breathed it in deeply and took the butter out of the refrigerator.

"Do you want to have breakfast, Mom?"
Very early, but for me the best time for breakfast. The bread would often still be a little bit warm. Which is good because the butter melts on the slices. Quince jelly and tea on the side. "Later I want to do the same thing with my kids," my son said recently. "I can already make tea and I'm going to learn how to bake bread!"

Life is clever.
It makes a gift of these moments which flood us with happiness. My son and I could even smell happiness. Happiness which can be cut into slices.

135

"The kids were really nice."

"I know, I like them a lot too."

"Really very very nice kids."

"What's up with you Vitus? You're so sentimental."

"I would love to have children."

"Cute little sourdough boys and girls?"

"You have no respect."

"No, I've just got a sense of humor."

"Do you want to know how sourdough makes kids?"

"I'm not sure I want to find out."

"Sourdough multiplies through germinating power."

"Please spare me the details."

"Thanks! You really know how to put the brakes on a conversation."

"We're almost there. Please be good and on your best behavior. Vitus?"

WISDOM

GOOD IS ALWAYS NOW

To be able to see beautiful things ...

and to never stop enjoying them.

That is the wisdom of the heart.

Patricia Riekel is the queen of people journalism. She has interviewed pop icons and kings and propelled magazines out of the circulation basement to unimagined heights.
But she had never baked sourdough bread before. For her, sourdough was a baking ingredient sold in organic food stores in squishy bags.
She is accustomed to fearlessly tackling new challenges. Especially when she knows that the beginning could be shaky. Someone like Patricia Riekel delivers what she intends to do, and that's why I'm not worried when I make an appointment with her. An appointment for a sourdough baking day!

When I stop working so hard, I'll bake you bread every day! Such a huge promise!
A promise one of Germany's most successful journalists made to her husband. She mentions it when we meet in her office.
Up until now her life has been determined by deadlines and circulation figures. The miles of red carpet she's walked on are incalculable. Her baby is *Bunte*, Europe's largest people magazine. Editor-in-chief for 20 years, then publisher. She's never had any time. But now she's given up all of her duties and is reorganizing her life …

"I want to bake him bread which really smells like bread!"
"Sourdough bread smells very bready!"
"He likes bread which is soft inside and has a real crust outside."
"That sounds like sourdough bread."
"The crust has to taste good as well, not just crunch!"
"Exactly! That's sourdough!"
"Great, then I'll bake sourdough tomorrow. Where do I get the sourdough?"
"The best way is to make it yourself."
"Good, then I'll do it myself!"

I was very curious as I drove to her house by Lake Starnberg. Her husband had been my teacher at journalism school. Helmut Markwort, a famous man. I loved to hear him speak because his language was so beautiful—and I admired her sensational ascent. We had occasionally met each other over the years. I liked her naturalness.

"She's difficult," others said. "Come on, somebody who wants everybody to love her can't produce a successful magazine," I said.

One day an indignant colleague told me that a letter had gone around at the magazine *Bunte* which instructed everyone not to throw away paper on which only one side had been written on, but to also use the blank reverse side for notes. That's when she won my heart entirely.

The drive from Munich to Lake Starnberg is a gift in itself. I'm always surprised at how close the mountains are. Farmhouses right and left. I would love to take a peek inside many of them.

Our date is for 2 p.m. I have enough time to take a detour to a mill because I love the smell of flour and I want to pick up some kind of lovely, vintage grain. Maybe einkorn wheat, emmer or kamut. The recipe we've planned to use calls for wheat but an old-fashioned grain would certainly be nicer. I even find a real rarity: purple wheat and a miller who loves to pass on his knowledge. He tells me that purple wheat has a nutty flavor, is full of protein and results in pink-colored flour due to the grain's violet shell. I buy two one-kilo bags.

**"You can't miss my house,"
Patricia Riekel had told me.**
"It looks like a house in New England." The description is perfect. The front door is open. "Come on in!" someone calls from inside. The doors to the terrace are also open. A little bit of a draught is pleasant on such a hot day. The wooden planks of the floor are painted white and the lake is visible through the windows. I feel like I'm at the beach on the Long Island Sound where I spend a couple of weeks each summer.

The lady of the house is wearing a cotton dress and sneakers and laughs as she comes to meet me. I had asked her if I should bring along a make-up artist for the photos. This is not unusual, many people feel more comfortable when a pro takes care of the make-up and hair. "Nonsense!" she had answered. I'm overwhelmed by the view of the lake. "It must be a dream to write here," I say.

"That's exactly why I put my desk in the other room. If I look out the window, I can't look inside myself to write." A wise sentence. I'd never considered that before but it makes sense.

**"I've reserved the entire day
for our sourdough," she says.**
Shall we take a quick tour before we start baking?"
She doesn't have to ask me twice. In the meantime, Vitus definitely won't bubble out of his jar. He is resting in his well-tempered cooler.

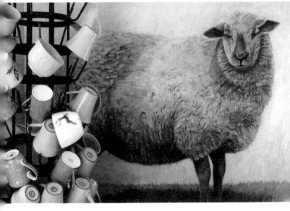

There is nothing off the rack in this house.

A lot of white. Hamptons-white! The bathroom is a girl's dream; the ceiling in the bedroom is covered in clouds painted by a friend of hers. The narrow room leading to the terrace is furnished with armchairs upholstered in velvet in a favorite color. Turquoise like a mermaid's eyes.

"Over time, the surroundings color your soul!" she says, because she's happy that I take delight in what I see. Based on the colors in this house, a friendly, bright soul lives here.

The kitchen is open to the living and dining rooms.

There are enough cups to provide an entire school class with tea and the number of dining room chairs would allow them all to sit down. Patricia Riekel is a sourdough beginner. "What did I do wrong?" she asks and opens up a plastic container. Her very first attempt at making sourdough starter is floating around inside. It's wearing a moldy, turquoise-colored cap. At least it's in her favorite color, but it can't be saved.

Sometimes just a small tip helps to solve a huge problem.

Plastic containers are namely unsuited for preparing starter. Jars are better because smaller openings offer fewer possibilities for mold spores to enter. Patricia Riekel's second sourdough starter looks good. It's bubbling gently but at least it's bubbling. She had informed herself. Research is in her blood. But the first bread still wasn't a big hit. "The first dough was just a lumpy thing. Although I followed the recipe. I called a friend who can really bake bread. But he wasn't a big help. Men put dough together as if they were building a car!" She laughs and spoons the failed first attempt onto the compost.

"Sourdough is a miracle to me. Water and flour ... and then all of a sudden it's alive. It's almost spooky!"

We arrange everything we'll need for baking. We agree on using the purple wheat, and Vitus can finally come out of his thermos. Patricia Riekel writes down everything new that she learns, asks lots of questions and sometimes chuckles with joy. "I think sourdough is really sensuous. There's life inside. I'm completely awestruck."

She still kneads and folds hesitantly but her intuition is good and she delights in the dough's sour fragrance.

Once Vitus is placed into the banneton and set to work to puff up the purple wheat sourdough, we decide to sit down on the mermaid-eye-colored armchairs and talk. But first we want to go down to the lake. It's only a few steps away.

Sourdough conversations could turn into my favorite kinds of conversations.

The dough takes its time to rise and the people take their time to talk. A comfortable peace settles over the conversation. A small piece of the lake shore belongs to her alone. A hip-high garden gate separates the pebbly beach and the wooden dock from the narrow footpath in front of it.

Lake Starnberg! The fateful lake in which Bavaria's King Ludwig II drowned. The lake is her source of energy, she says. A giant blow-up swan, the fairy-tale king's heraldic animal, rocks on top of the water. Patricia Riekel has really made it. She may be unrivaled professionally but she's also held on to her humor and joy.

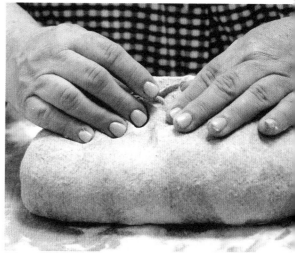

"I'd go a mile for butter bread!
I enjoy it more than a three-star meal. My husband just couldn't imagine life without bread."
The dough is developing wonderfully in its banneton. Vitus still has half an hour to jump-start the purple wheat bread.
"A slice of bread with cream cheese is a delicacy. Sometimes I think it would be nice to be thinner. But I no longer even ask myself if five kilos on the hips are too many. Bread makes me beautiful on the inside and then that radiates on the outside!"

The dough is put into the hot pot.
The purple wheat has lent it the pinkish color of a marzipan pig. 500 °F in the oven turns it into bread and in the meantime, Vitus is fed. With purple wheat and honey water. "Working with you is to discover slowness. Every movement suddenly has meaning," writes Patricia Riekel in Vitus's travel diary. "I hope you will be as treasured everywhere as you are here by Lake Starnberg!"

PURPLE WHEAT BREAD

600 g purple wheat flour or wheat flour
250 g whole grain spelt flour
100 g whole grain rye flour
½ tsp sugar
10 g fresh yeast
110 g sourdough starter
550 g warm water
1 tbsp honey
20 g soft butter
15 g salt

Put approximately 100 g of the warm water into each of two small dishes. Dissolve the yeast with the sugar in one dish and stir the honey into the second dish. Put all the other ingredients except the salt into the bowl of a food processor, then add the honey-water mixture and the dissolved yeast and knead everything on the slowest speed for 4–5 minutes. Add the salt, raise the speed of the food processor to the next highest speed and knead for a further 8–10 minutes. Cover the dough and leave to rise in the bowl. It should be allowed to rest for a total of 90 minutes, but with interruptions during which it should be stretched and folded—the first time after 30 minutes and again after 60 minutes.

After 90 minutes form the dough into an oval on the floured work surface and lay it into the banneton with the seam underneath. Cover and leave to rise for 60 minutes. Bake the bread according to the casserole method. Heat the oven and the casserole to 500 °F, remove the lid and slip the loaf from the banneton into the hot casserole. For this recipe the bread should be left in the oven for 45 minutes at the same temperature (500 °F). Then tip onto a rack and leave to cool.

WISE AND SALTY!

Salt is a bubble chiller.

Sourdough respects punctuality. So do I, just not on Sunday mornings. With the exception of a hungry kitty, almost nothing can give you such a look of reproach as sourdough that wants to be released from its overnight proofing basket. I've recently started adding a teaspoon of salt to the dough to ensure that I get a goodnight's sleep. Used wisely it slows down the sourdough's rising process.

Most of the recipes call for salt at the end so that the fermentation doesn't come to a halt too soon. But it can work the other way around as well: Add salt to the dough at the beginning in order to slow it down. That way the dough can rest longer and so can you.

Salt is a cosmetic for pots.

Everybody loves the pot method and they all wonder why the bread just pops out of the pot without even a drop of oil being used beforehand. If the bread doesn't pop out, it's because the pot wasn't hot enough or it had been over-zealously cleaned. The grease solvents in dishwashing liquids namely "tear" the invisible film which acts as a natural non-stick coating.

Cast-iron roasting pans don't need anything other than salt and oil. "Massage" the inside of the pot with common table salt and olive oil using a soft cloth. Remove the salt-oil mixture and wipe with a damp cloth. I recommend using coarse salt and elbow grease for the really hard cases! The effort is worth it because you can bring even totally worn out cast-iron pots and pans from thrift shops and flea markets back to life.

Salt flatters your hands.

Whoever decides to bake bread mustn't be afraid of getting their hands dirty. But it's good to know how to get them clean again. How about a paste which not only cleans, but beautifies as well? Coarse salt is not only good for the pots, but also for your hands. And together with a bit of dishwashing liquid, you can mix up the "hobby baker's favorite hand-washing paste." How? Put coarse salt in a jar and fill it up with enough dishwashing liquid until the salt is covered. That's it! The paste keeps for months. If you make enough in reserve, your doughy fingers will be clean in a wink. It also makes a great present!

BREAD ENHANCERS

I love simple bread recipes. They are a fine basis for your own bread creations. As soon as we have a sourdough starter at the ready, one which we trust, we can knead our way through every recipe without losing our nerve. And then the time is ripe to experiment a little.

Melted butter is a good substitute when a recipe calls for oil. Butter lures out new aromas. Add a few chopped walnuts and your delicious creation is finished.

Cashews and a **hint of saffron** are wonderful. They give bread a delicately tart taste, a lovely color and a crunchy bite.

Cranberries and **applesauce** are also terrific. They insert a tiny touch of sweetness which fits perfectly to the sourdough aroma. When using applesauce, be sparing with the water in the recipe.

Herbs are always good. **Rosemary**, dried or fresh, gives the bread a Mediterranean touch. **Parsley** crisply sautéed in hot oil and added to the bread dough is delicious because the pan roasting fires up the aromas of the parsley. **Dried savory, chives, oregano … all** superb natural bread enhancers.

Juices are also amazing in bread dough. The best come fresh out of the juicer. Store-bought juices are okay as long as they are unadulterated and sugar-free. The water in the recipe should be completely replaced by the juice or mixed with it.

Carrot juice is fantastic, red beet juice creates aroma and color and **apple or pear juice** support the sourdough to do its job due to their sweetness. But promise me you'll never try to use sauerkraut juice! Is it a promise? Good!

My absolutely favorite bread enhancer is commonly put on top of hot dogs. But this culinary task is far below the capabilities of this enhancer. It's found on supermarket shelves and produces with the smallest effort the greatest "Yummy!" in bread … I'm talking about sautéed onions. Ready-to-use out of the simple plastic container. A handful is enough to make a delicacy out of the simplest bread.

TIP
"Bavarian bread spice"
Bread spice is popular in Germany, Austria and Switzerland. The taste of anise, fennel and in particular caraway is generally found in standard Bavarian bread.
If you prefer a less classic taste, add some coriander seeds. The dry spices are mixed in equal amounts and finely ground in a food processor or a mortar. Whoever owns an old coffee grinder can be pleased because it works especially well here. A small portion of bread spice in the dough turns simple sourdough bread into "Bavarian Farmer's Bread"!

147

WAYS FOR KEEPING EVERYTHING FRESH

Sourdough can be preserved for an astoundingly long time. Sometimes, it even improves in aroma when it is older. But if the bread is stored in a place in which it can age with dignity, it has only two choices: get hard or get moldy.

Starch absorbs water during the bread baking process. This moisture escapes again when the bread is stored. That's why bread which is stored in plastic containers or bags in which the moisture is prevented from escaping becomes rubbery and at some point moldy. Bread which has completely lost its moisture becomes hard. You can only enjoy older bread when it has not been allowed to dry out or become chewy. Happy is the person who knows where bread feels most comfortable.

Clay pots can keep bread fresh for a long time. Clay is porous and can regulate the moisture level. I picked up my clay bread pots at the garden center. I take mostly large, untreated flower pots and paint them (on the outside!). The paint has to be breathable and free of noxious substances. Many chalk-based paints are suitable as are linseed oil paints. However, for the latter you need lots of patience as linseed oil paints dry very, very slowly.

Use a round kitchen chopping board to close the pot. Screw a chest of drawers' knob, which you can get at the hardware store, on the top. Finished! Lids from old cooking pot are also lovely. I can never resist a lonely lid at flea markets and yard sales. This reserve of lids allows me to construct my own bread pot whenever I want, which I can then give as a present together with a loaf of freshly baked bread.

Enamel is also good. There are containers in many forms and colors. Good enamel is a fantastic material. Old enamel cooking pots are especially fitting as bread boxes. Their lids shut tightly but they are not totally airtight and enamel can be cleaned in the dishwasher without problem. If you wrap your bread in linen cloth before you put it into an enamel box, you'll achieve the absolutely best results.

Linen sacks get along well with bread and a kitchen door, on which a linen bread bag can be hung, must be available to everybody. I find the most beautiful linen sacks at Bavarian flea markets. Why is linen so good to bread? Because it can absorb moisture and prevent the bread from becoming mushy.

Swiss pinewood (bot. *Pinus cembra*) boxes are still an insider's tip for storing bread. Swiss pine grows in the Alps. It secretes pinosylvin, an aromatic substance which is anti-bacterial and helps to prevent mold formation in bread. Swiss pine can additionally, similar to clay, absorb moisture and release it again under dry conditions. In other words, the ideal prerequisites for the best bread boxes. Small carpenters' workshops in the region of the Alps produce such *Zirbenholz* boxes by hand.* And what do you do if you don't have room for a bread box in your kitchen? No problem, there are also solutions for the small kitchen.

Robust types of bread with thicker crusts keep fresher longer even without a box! Sourdough bread is one of the frontrunners in terms of the bread preservability. High rye content and a lot of whole grain increase the lifespan of the bread even more. Whole grain breads can be eaten for up to nine days. Simply place the cut surface of the bread face down onto a wooden board and cover with a dish towel.

TIP
Bread boxes of every sort should be washed out from time to time with vinegar water. Vinegar is a natural and effective remedy against mold.

"Did you hear that? I'm appreciated! And by everyone!"

"Up until now everyone's been incredibly nice to you."

"Forget nice. Why do I have to work the whole time while you get to take a stroll along the lake?"

"Because you're made of acetic acid and lactic acid and I'm not."

"You only see my bubbles but I want to be loved for my whole self."

"Calm down, otherwise you're going to bubble over. In my eyes you're the greatest!"

"Really?"

"You're cooperative, handsome, you do a good job, you smell good and take up hardly any space in the fridge."

"Can I have that in writing?"

"You're going to get a present at the end of our journey, that's even better!"

"Do I still have to wait long?"

"Just a little bit longer, but right now you're going to have some beer."

"Beer?"

"Beer!"

TRANQUILITY

BREAD BEATS BETA-BLOCKERS

To eat breakfast above the roofs of a city with a thousand-year history.
So beautiful!

To enjoy a brioche on porcelain fit for a museum. What a treasure!

To bake bread with beer from the oldest brewery in the world. Delicious!

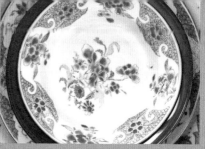

Books, paintings, recipes, plates, cups …
Everything in this house breathes history. Only Josef Sellmair's history is contemporary. It speaks about breaking down barriers in the mind and about a life which has been shaken to its core.

When Josef bakes bread, 16 grams mean 16 grams.
Not just "a pinch" and not "more or less a teaspoon." Josef doesn't bake using his intuition. Everything is weighed with precision. With precision scales. And when the timer goes off, everything else stops. Immediately! No "let me just quickly clear out the dishwasher" or "I'll just write this one e-mail!" When the timer announces the next ignition stage for the dough, hands are instantly dipped into cold water and the "stretching and folding" begins. Josef can set the table, fill up the dishwasher, juggle red current jam from a jar into a

porcelain bowl and talk on the phone. Not one thing after the other. All at the same time! Yet when Josef bakes bread everything is calm, exact and done in sequence. Like clockwork. Step by step. Every movement seems relaxed. When he bakes, even the bowls clatter more quietly when he places them onto the tabletop.

Saturday is baking day. Every Saturday for three years.
Bread for the entire week. To start with, just because it was delicious and then as a countermeasure against the many "I have-tos" which nag him on Saturdays. "I have to do my taxes," "I have to paint the bathroom." … Nasty little whisperers who have what it takes to ruin every weekend. Josef Sellmair is a member of a traditional Bavarian family company which makes bathrobes and nightwear. Stress from Monday to Friday. But ever since Josef became acquainted with sourdough, the fragrance of fresh crusts has cleared away the tension. Or, as Josef would say: "The smell of bread is better than beta-blockers."

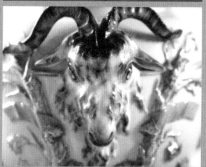

153

The refrigerator is brimming with delicious things.
Jars take up a quarter of the space. Sourdough starters. Each one carefully labelled. Josef not only has one, but many. Nobody would be able to find the butter in this refrigerator. Nobody but Josef. He knows without looking that it is behind the double row of sourdough jars. Right next to the camembert. A bag of peaches is lying on the table. And cherries. They'll be used for the photographs and later for breakfast and they need to be carried upstairs.

The man of the house grips a tablecloth and the matching napkins under his arm.
He puts the fruit and the butter onto a tray. A knife, a vase and a stack of porcelain plates. Plates this precious usually are displayed behind glass, in Josef's house, they are used. The peaches roll around on the tray as he walks. The plates clatter alarmingly and the cherries start to slide. I don't want to think about how I'd explain it to my insurance company if this stack of plates turned into shards of broken porcelain. Because I'm the one responsible for encouraging the man of the house to take a few photos in the upstairs rooms.

Josef told me that he revered the French painter Jean-Siméon Chardin.
And because his favorite still-life by Chardin is needed in the Louvre in Paris, he went to a copy shop and had it reproduced onto canvas. An extremely appetizing scene from 1763 of fruit and a liqueur next to a loaf of sweet bread into which a spray of orange blossoms has been inserted.
I had an idea and wanted to carefully win Josef over to it.
"Josef, is it true that you read old French cookbooks?"
"Yes, I enjoy doing that."

"Even old baking books?"
"Yes, if I can find some. They are rarer than the cookbooks!"
"Could you bake such old-fashioned, sweet bread?"
"Do you mean like a brioche?"
"Yes. A kind of white bread with a pom-pom on top. If you could bake a loaf which looked like the one in the painting, then we could set up our own living Chardin."

We take the printed Chardin off its hook, set it onto a sideboard and lean it against a green wall.
It takes a while until we've found the right porcelain bowl. Not because we couldn't find a similar one. Just the opposite: the selection was too large. Josef collects porcelain from the 18th century. Plates, terrines, candy bowls. Unique and precious. We drape the fruit and the liqueur, and as we finally find the right bowl for the left edge of the photograph, Josef brings the brioche out of the kitchen.

It wasn't so easy to bake a brioche which looked like a twin to Chardin's brioche.
Josef not only wanted to bake sweet bread which looks like the Parisian brioche from 1763. He also wanted to bake it in the same way as in 18th-century France. "A mountain of butter and lots of eggs," says Josef. That hasn't changed even today. But how much of each ingredient? There wasn't any metric system in 18th-century cookbooks." Josef, the man with the precision scales, had to fiddle around, but the result

is gratifying and tasty. The brioche was eaten for breakfast after the "living Chardin" had been documented for all eternity. Mild, sweet bread which could become addictive. "In the past, the painters even used white bread as erasers!" "The painters did what?" "They not only ate their white bread, but they used it to erase pencil strokes. Erasers were invented only in 1770," laughs Josef.
This man is not only a baker; he's a walking encyclopedia.

155

A breakfast which could have stepped out of the 18th century is something special.
So is bringing a painting from the Louvre to life on a Bavarian sideboard, but I wanted to persuade Josef to bake another kind of bread. He is an unusually helpful man and very sponta-neous. I was certain that he'd like my idea.

The little city in which Josef lives is called Freising and it is located in Bavaria.
Not far from Munich. Resting upon two hills. On one of them is a very famous cathedral. Ancient. On the other is a still more famous brewery. Even older! It is the oldest brewery in the world.
"Josef, I think Vitus is mature enough for his first beer. He's had so many good things … honey, elderflower syrup, holy water. He could manage a beer now."

I actually had a plan.
It's a custom in Bavarian beer gardens for guests to get their beer at the tap and then look for a shady spot under the densest trees. A picnic basket also comes along. Many years ago a Bavarian monarch issued a decree which allowed you for all eternity to bring your own picnic basket to a beer garden.

The only condition: You have to buy a beer from the proprietor. Today you're also allowed to buy water or soft drinks.

"Can you bake hearty bread, Josef?

Bread in which you can taste Vitus when you bite into it and which goes with cheese and radishes."

"You just want to go up the hill to the Weihenstephan brewery, isn't that right?"

"Exactly, and with a picnic basket, and then we'll sit down in the beer garden and have a snack and a good beer!"

That's how Josef came to bake his "Freising Beer Bread." Hearty and crusty and made with beer from the oldest brewery in the world. Baked with precisely weighed ingredients and exact-to-the-minute stretching and folding.

Perhaps Josef values the precise procedure of bread baking so much because he has experienced how life follows other rules.

We often think that if we precisely weigh up our actions, our expectations in life will be met with the same degree of accuracy. That might work in baking bread. Life often has other plans. Josef was married for many years and is the father of three wonderful children. His marriage dissolved and he was left alone. He has now been living with Georg for five years. A happy life. A life which was first shaken down to its foundations but now feels precisely right.

FREISING BEER BREAD

Predough

70 g whole grain rye flour
70 g hot water
70 g sourdough starter
Mix well and leave to rest for
6–8 hours at room temperature.

After 5–7 hours make a second dough

560 g wheat flour
350 g beer (can also be alcohol-free beer or water)
This dough is a so-called auto-lysis dough. Cover and leave to rest for 1 hour.

When both doughs have developed sufficiently put them in the bowl of the food processor together with
16 g wheat flour
15 g active baking malt
15 g salt
70 g beer (can also be alcohol-free beer or water)
10 g yeast if required
Knead for 5 minutes at the lowest speed, then raise the speed to the next level and knead for a further 5 minutes.
Put the dough in an oiled bowl and leave to mature for 3 hours at room temperature.

Stretch and fold four times every 30 minutes.

Then form the dough into a round loaf and place in the banneton with the seam underneath. Leave to rise for another 1 hour. Bake the bread according to the casserole method. Heat the oven to 500 °F. Tip the dough into the casserole with the seam on top, cover with the lid and bake at 500 °F. After 25 minutes remove the lid and reduce the temperature to 450 °F. Bake for another 25 minutes. Tip the bread out, use the knocking test to check that it is cooked, and leave to cool on a rack.

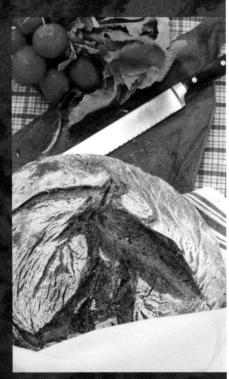

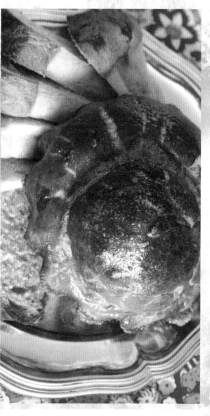

BRIOCHE À LA CHARDIN

70 g sourdough starter
500 g wheat flour
75 ml cream
12 g salt
6 eggs
300 g butter

Mix all the ingredients except the butter and blend for 5 minutes in the food processor on the lowest speed.

Then knead in the processor for a further 10–15 minutes until a firm dough is formed.

Add the butter in small pieces and knead for a further 5 minutes until the fat has been completely worked into the dough.

Cover the dough and leave to rise in the refrigerator for 2 hours. Stretch and fold the dough after 30 minutes and again after one hour.

Then form the brioche: divide the dough into two pieces, one small than the other, and form into a large and a small round ball. Place the small ball on top of the large one, cover and leave to rise overnight in the refrigerator. Preheat the oven to 450°F, paint the brioche with egg yolk and either place it directly in the oven or put it in a buttered form. Bake for 15–20 minutes.

POWER POWDER

Some recipes don't place their trust in the energy of sourdough alone but take it up a notch.
They recommend adding a kind of turbocharger to the bread dough: baking malt. Baking malt is a grain which is germinated and then dried, roasted and ground. The result is malt sugar, for which the microbes in sourdough have an enormous appetite. And because well-fed microbes puff up the dough particularly well, fermentation is also given an extra kick. There are a variety of baking malts. Active and inactive. Malt extract, black malt and malt flakes.

I only have the so-called "active baking malt" in my baking drawer.
Adding active baking malt to the dough is a "can" and not a "must." It generally stimulates fermentation specifically during final proofing and the oven rise, and it turns the crust a lovely crispy brown.

More is more is the wrong approach with baking malt.
Two percent of the entire amount of flour is the perfect dosage. Too much active baking malt promotes the increased production of starch during fermentation which leads to a glutinous, soggy dough.
By the way, if there is a lot of rye flour in the dough, you should do without active baking malt altogether.

Active baking malt is no cure-all.
Similar to the water wings yeast, active baking malt is a tool for supporting the sourdough. A strong sourdough starter like Vitus actually doesn't need any additional assistance. If you want to do something good for your starter, then fire it up from time to time with a teaspoon of honey or syrup. It will stay big and strong and will manage diverse amounts of dough all by itself.

HANDS VERSUS APPLIANCES

Whoever bakes bread has to work the dough.
Some dough is kneaded, some others are stretched and folded. Some more, some less. In short: anybody who wants to bite into fluffy bread has to treat the dough well.
Most of us will leave the handling of the dough up to a food processor. But which way is the best? Handheld mixers are eliminated for being too weak, because bread dough is heavy. What, then, are the right helpers in order to produce good bread dough?

Stand mixers

A good stand mixer has to be strong. Before you buy one, read the product description to see how much flour it can handle. It should be at least one kilo. A sturdy dough hook should be standard equipment. I prefer to work with the good old KitchenAid. Many bread doughs have to be kneaded for several minutes in the machine. Some other brands just can't take it. Even my KitchenAid sometimes heats up when it's kneading a large amount of dough for a longer period, but it never breaks down!*

Food processor

This appliance is a once-in-a-lifetime purchase and truly multi-talented. If you want fresh dinner rolls or you frequently eat waffles, or pancakes, a food processor is for you. It can knead small amounts of dough. Put in the flour, add water, close the lid, switch it on, done! It can't manage large amounts of dough for really big loaves of bread, but it can easily undertake nearly all other kitchen activities.**

Hands

Everything that a machine has to be painstakingly programmed to do our hands can do naturally. We can leave the heavy job of mixing flour and liquids to electrical appliances without a guilty conscience because they truly can't be beat. It's important to knead for a long time in order to distribute the gluten like a net throughout the dough. This loosens up the dough. But as soon as a lovely, elastic lump of dough emerges, our hands clearly hold the advantage.
The dough is placed onto a floured work surface and stretched and folded. This is the phase in which the dough is make ready to turn into good bread—and this really only happens by hand.

161

"Are you just writing that or do I truly make you happy?"

"You truly make me happy!"

"Why?"

"Because I like to watch you bubble and because you make my bread so delicious."

"Well why do you have to write a whole book about it? Can't you just enjoy your happiness in silence?"

"I think you've got what it takes to make a lot of people happy."

"Is that the truth?"

"That's the truth! And besides, everybody loves to eat yummy bread. Except my friend Diana."

"Then I don't want to meet her."

"You don't have to. Now we're traveling to meet someone who loves you just as much as I do."

"Maybe even a little bit more?"

"Possibly still a little bit more. He wants to paint you."

"You're kidding, aren't you?"

"I'm not kidding. A real sourdough portrait!"

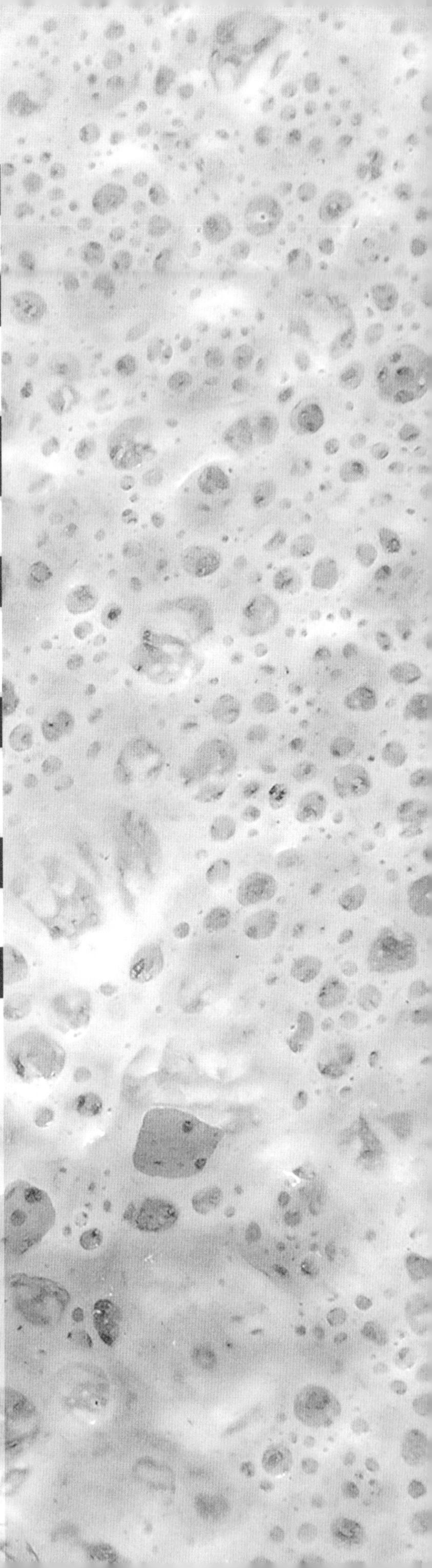

SIMPLICITY

EVERY SLICE IS A THING OF BEAUTY

The bread from Maine has many ingredients: Vitus, fresh blueberries, a portion of maple syrup, flour, salt and a painter's personal signature.

My friend John is a man of many talents.

He finds treasures which others can't see. He can fish, cook, and mount wheels onto the bottom of canoes. He can grow gigantic pumpkins, speak about three sentences in German and take care of Brazilian street kids. He can balance spoons on his nose, play a little bit of violin, and best of all, he can paint pictures. Pictures in which you can lose yourself.

"John, can you also bake bread?" I asked him in an e-mail.

I wanted to be careful not to cling to an idea which might amount to nothing.

"I love to bake bread," he wrote back almost immediately.

That was a start, but I wanted more.

"Can you also bake sourdough?"

"Sourdough is fabulous," he answered. "But I haven't baked with it for a long time."

I have a jar on my kitchen table. Vitus lives inside.

I looked at the air bubbles he produced. Over and over and always different. I observed his fine coloring: pink from purple wheat, a delicate gray from Pablo's rye flour, honey beer, elderflower syrup … everything together had turned him a golden vanilla.

Barbara had photographed him beautifully countless times, and I had shot a Polaroid photo of him at the end of every trip for my bulletin board. But there was only one person in my opinion who could capture Vitus's beauty forever.

"John, could you paint a loaf of sourdough bread for me?"

John liked my idea.

I imagined him sitting for many days in his studio at the easel. The room would be still. Now and again you would hear a seagull flying in from the sea, or the old floorboards squeaking when his wife Ellen brings him a coffee. The stillness would be broken only three or four times a week by the freight train which cuts through John's garden on its way to the cement factory. I imagined how John would paint Vitus. Every bubble would be painted finely and true to life, like the eyelashes of someone in the paintings of the Old Masters.

"When are you coming? Should I start up some sourdough?" he asked.

"Don't bother, I'm bringing one along. A particularly nice one. You'll like him."
"Don't you think that bread also should be in the painting? Sourdough bread?"
"Absolutely. I just didn't dare to ask," I responded and added five Smileys after the sentence. "I'm really excited about an original John Whalley with sourdough and bread!"

John loves bread.

It's impossible to go out to dinner with him and just thoughtlessly munch on the side order of bread. "Bread is so welcoming," he says. A charming description which can only be inadequately translated.

John appreciates every pore in the bread. He sees the sun glinting in the creamy yellow of the melting butter. In every restaurant in the US you're given dinner rolls to eat. A moment which makes John pause. He is thankful for the warm bread. A feeling which never seems to wear off.

Pemaquid Lobster Coop and, as a rule, I pull over to the side of the road shortly before arriving at my destination in order to buy a bottle of "Moxie." Moxie is the official soft drink of Maine. It tastes like cough syrup with Fanta and burns in your mouth for several minutes. As I lean against my car with a bottle of Moxie in my hand, the feeling of home wells up inside me.

I thought of all the many paintings of John's that I was familiar with.
Fascinating portraits, landscapes and the innumerable objects of daily life. Humble, abandoned things. A measuring spoon, an old paintbrush, a cookbook. But I could only remember one painting which included bread. I was present when it was finished.

An Indian art collector wanted John to paint him the Last Supper. John requested complete artistic freedom and he drew the street kids of Goias—the street kids with whom he had lived for many years. He painted Henrique, Tales and Gabriel. Every face at the table is a real face. The bread is in the middle. Every day it is a battle for survival for the young boys, every supper possibly their last.

John wrote that he had found a few other things in his studio.
Things which would go well with sourdough. He had put together a composition and was certain that I would like it. I was also certain that I would, so I prepared my trip.
Maine is on the East Coast of the US. I've spent many summers there. I usually fly to Boston and rent a car. I already get excited on the plane about driving Route 1 north. There is always a traffic jam in Ogunquit but I can use it to pick up some chocolate cookies from "Bread and Roses." I imagine the first lobster roll I'll eat at the

John and Ellen Whalley's house is painted my favorite color.
White! Like most of the houses on the East Coast. White and made of wood. When you enter through the front door you find yourself without warning directly in the kitchen. Open the door! Kitchen! How cozy! I was really looking forward to a coffee and my sourdough urgently needed to be fed so as not to become more sour than necessary. Vitus should show his best side to the man who would paint his portrait.

I still can remember the exact day on which I first entered this house.
Ellen's kitchen felt so familiar, as if I had grown up there. We sat down at the table in front of the window. Then I was allowed to visit John's studio.
The pictures that I saw touched me in a strange way. They filled me with the desire to embrace each image.
A myriad of objects were arranged along the dozens of shelves. Sorted according to size and color. Bottles in many shades of blue, lanyards, marmalade jars, ancient books, photographs and violins. A discarded rowboat underneath a blanket. Every object looked loved. This studio was the object orphanage of an artist who adopted abandoned things in order to give them a new home in his paintings.

Later, when John went on the hunt for new treasures, I was often along.
Saturdays and Sundays at the Montsweag flea market in Wiscasset or in the thrift shop of the Miles Memorial Hospital in Damariscotta. I watched fascinated as he examined discarded tools and dented tin cans so that he could listen to their stories.
There is nobody who shows so much respect for worn out everyday objects. It's as if he is bowing down before the work which these things had done over the years. He calls it redemption.

It felt so good to be there again!

"Do you want to see how far I've gotten with our painting?" Ellen had already greeted me by handing over a large cup of coffee. She knows me well and understands my craving after a long drive. I took a big sip and excitedly followed the artist to his studio.

John had chosen a loaf of bread, a castaway baking sheet, a Bible and an ancient barrel. He had placed a marmalade jar from

Ellen's kitchen in the middle. The jar was still empty. "Everything I wanted for our painting I found here in the studio, because I had picked it up at some point at a flea market," laughed John. "The only fresh thing is the bread from Borealis in Waldoboro. Good, handmade sourdough bread."

The painting was wonderful.

Everything absolutely authentic. It seemed as if you could smell the fresh crust. "It's only good when it's finished," said John, curbing my enthusiasm, "and it still needs loads of brushstrokes." I fetched the thermos in which Vitus sat in his jar. "We desperately need to feed him. He needs lots of energy to bubble and fill up the giant jar you want to paint him in!" I told John. As soon as Vitus had reached the right height in the jar, John could start working on his portrait. And I would watch over my favorite painter's shoulder while he did it.

169

John Whalley grew up in New York.

In Brooklyn with its dark rows of brownstone houses. For a long time, John couldn't even visualize green, blue or red. "I thought that there were only two colors in the world: brown and black." Only when his parents started to spend the weekends with their children in the countryside did he see flowers and trees and discovered colors.

He studied painting in Rhode Island. Art dealers and galleries quickly took notice of him. He could easily have lived from his painting but he went to South America in order to help street kids. Back in the US, he couldn't forget the children's misery. He goes to Brazil. There's a ranch there where street kids can go to school and get to know a life of security. John teaches the kids to paint and cooks for them. "We were often completely broke and we had to beg for flour from the country mills. I have never forgotten how precious flour is!"

John sat at his easel in his studio every day.

His patience with Vitus's tons of bubbles was limitless and when he painted, it was just as quiet in the studio as I had imagined it would be! Just not when John and I talked to each other.

John described what he had cooked for the Brazilian kids. "When we were out of everything, then at least we still had flour. And when we had flour, I could provide the children with bread."

John spent nearly six years on the ranch. Helped to give the children a home. His sons, Ben and Matthew, were with him. They grew up like brothers to the Brazilian boys. "Many of the street kids had experienced terrible things. I wanted to help them get back their dignity." For many of them, their way in life was made smoother thanks to the project. They learned trust and received an education. John has never completely left. Once a year he drums up American donors and guarantees that the kids are provided with bread for several months.*

"The first breads you baked probably tasted horrible and the kids ate them because you're so nice."

John laughed out loud. I took that as a "yes" and continued watching as he mixed the paints for the Vitus portrait. Every day from the beginning. Out of pigments and egg yolks. How he applies it layer by layer until the colors of bread, Bible, board and sourdough are exactly the way he wants them.

When John composes a picture, he often studies the objects for weeks at a time. He wants to see how light and shadow play with them. "It's like with an old radio with a dial. Sometimes it takes a while until you've found a good station and then longer until you can hear it clearly. That's more or less the moment when I can start to paint."

John worked every day on Vitus's portrait.

Although I'd already seen so many of John's paintings, I never failed to be amazed at the precision of his brush in painting details. When I wasn't watching him, I canvassed the Saturday garage sales with Ellen. We frequently ate homemade pickles at Morse's Sauerkraut and savored Moxies and sandwiches at Fernald's Country Store. Now and again we drove to Elmer's Barn in Coopers Mills and I looked forward every morning to the blueberry pancakes at the Mill Pond Inn in Nobleboro.

And then finally the painting was finished.
A big moment. John had painted wonderfully. Pure and magnificent at the same time. He had captured all of the gratitude he felt for bread. John Whalley, the painter from Maine, who was incapable of throwing away even a slice. Not even

when it had become as hard as the leg of a chair.
"What do you think if I bake our farewell bread with blueberries and maple syrup from Maine—and Vitus, of course?" I thought it was a terrific idea.
While the blueberry bread rose in the oven, John prepared Vitus for his trip home. At least it had

to seem that way to Vitus, because he had no idea that a surprise was in store for him. John fed him with organic wheat flour from Maine and water from the well underneath his house, and we winked at each other because we both knew that our goodbyes were not going to happen immediately.

The bread John had baked was heavenly.

Sweet with the maple syrup, fruity because of the blueberries and fluffy thanks to Vitus. "Look at that," John said. "Every loaf of bread is a work of art, and when you cut into it, every slice is a thing of beauty."

It was sentences like these which gave me the idea months ago to ask John to bake me a sourdough painting. I'm happy I asked him. "Bread is life," John had said at our first meeting. "Bread truly is life. I really love this meaning!" So do I, John. So do I!

johnwhalley.com

173

BLUEBERRY BREAD FROM MAINE

100 g sourdough starter
300–400 g lukewarm water
300 g wheat flour
175 g whole grain wheat flour
10 g salt
100–125 g maple syrup
250 g blueberries

Mix all the ingredients except the maple syrup and the blueberries in a bowl. Cover and leave to rest for 2 hours. Put the dough on a floured board. At the beginning it will be fairly sticky and will only start to take shape after four rounds of "stretch and fold." Each round will take 3–5 minutes, then put the dough back in the bowl. Cover and leave to rest for 15 minutes. Repeat the entire process four times. Then form the dough into a rectangle on a lightly floured board. Do not add too much flour as the dough will not roll out properly if you do. Using a rolling pin, roll out the dough to the thickness of your finger, forming a large rectangle. Spread out the blueberries and the maple syrup and roll to make a "packet." First fold over a margin on the two short sides and then roll up the dough from the long side. Wrap the dough packet in a cloth and plastic film and leave it to rest in the refrigerator at least overnight. It should be left for at least 12 but not more than 24 hours. Before baking it should then be left to rest at room temperature for a further 1 to 2 hours. Bake the loaf at 450 °F for about 50 minutes. You can either bake it open in the oven—in which case you will need plenty of steam to ensure a good crust—or you can use the pot method. In this case the loaf should be baked for half the time with the lid on the pot, and then without the lid for the second half of the cooking time.

TIP
Instead of fresh blueberries you can also use frozen ones or blueberries from a jar. The latter must be well drained before use. The loaf is also delicious when made with cranberries or raisins. Both should be well soaked and then drained before use.

SOURDOUGH CAPS

Did I already mention that things sometimes used to get very hot in my parents' marital bed?
Especially when my mother left the house at lunchtime and was not expected back until the late evening. On those days the temperature rose dramatically between the mattress and the duvet, especially at the foot of the bed. My mother used to put the pan containing the mashed potatoes in the bed. She covered it carefully so that it would stay hot until my father came home from work. Please note: Things which are properly covered will not get cold.

Sourdough is highly offended when it is allowed to get cold—and it dislikes draughts even more.
Sourdough likes to puff itself up best of all at about 80 °F. My sourdough gets a cap on its head so that it doesn't suffer from cold air or fluctuating temperatures while it is rising in the bowl. The cap is usually even pre-warmed beforehand.

In my grandmother's days they used to be called tea cozies and they were used to keep tea or coffee hot.
I use my experience of these cozies for my sourdough. When used as sourdough caps they ensure that the sourdough can rise nicely without the need for electricity.
You can buy ready-made tea cozies. Unfortunately they are only big enough to cover up a jar of starter underneath them. It is much better to take a few strips of fabric and line them with fluffy fleece and then stitch them together to make a cap. And who do we call for when we need to sew something pretty? That's right! My friend Simone. I am known as a complete dyslexic when it comes to sewing. The most I could manage was to dye the old linen which Simone used to make the sourdough cap. A sourdough cap should be large enough so that the bowl fits comfortably underneath it. Before using the cap I put a pot of hot tea or coffee underneath. As soon as the cap is warm, I put it over the bowl or jar so that it can help the dough to rise.

I am very fond of simple tricks like the sourdough caps!
They can be put to work at any time without the use of electricity—and they are attractive to look at too.
And so to make all of the other "sewing dyslexics" happy, we can simply share my friend Simone. She has put the pattern for the sourdough cap on her website together with instructions which even I can understand.*

PUTTING DRY BREAD TO GOOD USE!

As we know, wasting good bread was once regarded as a sin. People who threw away bread would go straight to Hell immediately after they died. The idea of wasting good bread seems decidedly anachronistic nowadays, and Hell is pretty old-fashioned too. Perhaps that is the reason why more bread than ever lands in the trash today. In Europe alone, some three million tons of bread are thrown away every year. That would be enough to feed a medium-sized country all year round. Many bakeries and supermarkets ensure that stale bread is given to food programs or otherwise donated to charity. In private homes, however, far too much bread is still thrown away. I suggest making it into something tasty instead.

Bread chips
Cut the stale bread into slices that are as thin as possible. Chop a clove of garlic and stir it into some olive oil. Brush the slices of bread with the oil, sprinkle with Fleur de Sel and bake golden brown in the oven.

Burgers
Whatever you call them—burgers, meatballs, rissoles … in most regions of Germany they are usually made with rolls that have been soaked beforehand. Rolls are good, but a robust stale loaf will add more flavor. And it doesn't always have to be meat that you use! Salmon rissoles with soaked whole grain bread are delicious!

Savory baked bread
Grease a fireproof dish and fill with cubes of stale bread. Add some fried onions and then pour over a mixture of eggs and milk flavored with salt, pepper and grated cheese. Bake in the oven until golden brown.

Bread pudding
For bread pudding, mix some honey or sugar into the mixture of eggs and milk. Maple syrup is also excellent. Add some raisins or cranberries—and anyone who has tried the version with a few marshmallows between the cubes of bread will never throw stale bread away again.

Bread soup
My favorite recipe for using up stale bread is bread soup. People say it was invented by the peasants of South Tyrol. It involves virtually no cooking and for me it is the epitome of a good, simple meal. Bread up the pieces of stale bread (any kind will do) and bring it to the boil in meat or vegetable stock. Add some cream or crème fraîche, season with salt and pepper and puree using a handheld mixer or the food processor to make a creamy soup. Garnish with a few herbs or crisp onions … and the delicious meal is ready to serve.

A BACKUP COPY

A sourdough starter that has gone with us through the thickest and thinnest of bread-making experiences will eventually conquer a corner of our heart.
It doesn't bear thinking about that our beloved sourdough might one day catch a mold and end up in sourdough heaven. There is a helpful measure that is useful in case of the sudden demise of the sourdough: a backup! What? Like this!

Line a baking tray with baking paper and spread a thin layer of sourdough on the paper.
It must be a really thin layer and the starter must be really active and bubbly. Dry it at room temperature for about two days.

The sourdough is clearly dry when it is very light in color.
It will then be easy to separate it from the baking paper.

Now you can break it into coarse pieces, crumble it finely or grind it to powder.
Powder is especially practical. You can make the finest powdered sourdough in the food processor, but you can also crush it by hand in a pestle and mortar.

Dried sourdough starter should not be stored in an airtight container.
The best way is to use a preserving jar with a loosely-fitting lid. A greaseproof paper bag is also suitable.

And how do you reactivate the dried starter?
Some people just add it to the dough like dried yeast. I don't find this method particularly satisfactory.

Dried sourdough can easily be reactivated with water and flour:
1 part powdered starter
1 part lukewarm water
Stir and leave to stand for 2–3 hours.
Add 1 part flour—preferably whole grain flour.
Stir and leave to stand for 12 hours at room temperature.

The reactivated starter should start to bubble again. If not, feed it again and leave it for another 12 hours. Then it will be ready to face any sort of challenge.

TIP
Dried sourdough starter also makes an attractive gift for home bakers. Nicely packed in a jar and with a short description of how to activate it.
100 g of dried sourdough have slightly more than 300 calories, depending on which type of flour was used.

BREAD WITH AN IRISH SOUL

In the US you will find baking soda (bicarbonate of soda) in every kitchen.
It is used in almost everything that is supposed to rise in the oven and nonetheless remain moist inside.
Soda bread gets its name from baking soda. It is eaten on all holidays in deference to one's ancestors. These are the Irish ancestors which many American families have somewhere in their family tree.
Soda bread is as Irish as the shamrock—the three-leaved clover—or the potato.

Soda bread, the taste of which Irish immigrants carried with them in their hearts when they left their homeland, is touchingly easy to make.
In its original version it consists only of flour, salt, baking soda and sour milk …
In Germany you will find baking soda if you look for "Natron." The sourdough and the hint of honey and butter included in this recipe seem almost frivolous. But sourdough goes well with baking soda, because its acidity spurs it on and together with the buttermilk it will make the bread beautifully fluffy.

420 g whole grain wheat flour
1 tsp salt
1 tsp baking soda (bicarbonate of soda)
60 g butter
350 g sourdough starter
240 g buttermilk
1 tbsp honey
1 egg to glaze

Mix the flour, salt and baking soda in a bowl. Add the cold butter in small cubes and mix until the mixture is crumbly. Mix the liquid ingredients, the honey, buttermilk and sourdough starter, in a second bowl. Then combine the dry and wet ingredients and stir to form a smooth mixture. Tip the dough onto a floured work surface and knead for 20–30 minutes!
Make two round loaves and lay them on a baking sheet lined with baking paper.
Cut a cross in the top of each loaf and brush with beaten egg. Bake in a preheated oven at 350 °F for 35–45 minutes.

TIP
**I recommend eating Irish soda bread lukewarm, with salted butter and your eyes closed.
And here is a bonus tip for those who want to see something incredible:
According to an Irish tradition, you should rub a crushed clover leaf on your eyelids.
Why? Because then you will see a fairy island through your closed eyes.**

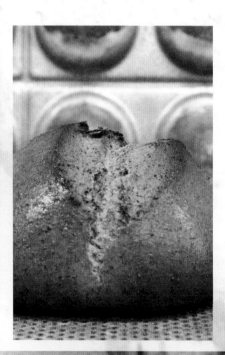

SURPRISES FOR VITUS

The end of my time with Vitus was approaching.

It was a good time, and I shall never forget the journey with him. Through various countries of Europe and then over here, to the Northeast of the United States.

Vitus and I had made bread with wonderful people and each time I was able to take more than a recipe back home with me. Each time there was also something that touched my soul as well. During the many months in which Vitus lived in my refrigerator he conquered my heart.

As a farewell gesture I had prepared a few surprises for Vitus which would change his sourdough life once and for all.

Karl De Smedt, the sourdough librarian from St. Vith, who had given us the right feeding instructions as the beginning of Vitus's sourdough life, was on his way to the US. He was not traveling alone but was also bringing his cameraman Rik. The two of them were going to make a film about the once unknown sourdough from Munich which had become the subject of a painting in Maine.

And so that Vitus could demonstrate his bubbling expertise in moving pictures, John would bake his wonderful blueberry bread for the second time with Karl. A place had also been reserved for Vitus in the famous Sourdough Library of Puratos in St. Vith. That is truly wonderful, because only very special sourdoughs are preserved for eternity in this library. After our trip to the US, I'm going to take Vitus to Belgium. A large jar bearing the number 101 has been reserved for him there.

John Whalley's sourdough painting will be carefully packed and sent to Europe, where it will also be given a place of honor in the Sourdough Library. It will be hung in a beautifully lit space within sight of Vitus, and in the future, bakers from all over the world will not only visit the Sourdough Library but will also be able to admire John's portrait of Vitus.

"Am I going to end up as a museum piece now?"

"Not a museum piece, Vitus. You're as fresh as a daisy."

"Who's going to feed me in the Sourdough Library?"

"Karl will do that in the future."

"Karl, who made the film with me at John's house?"

"Exactly! That Karl!"

"What if he doesn't stir as well as you do?"

"Karl will stir you really well. Are you starting to feel sad?"

"Sourdough doesn't have feelings."

"That's simply not true! When you're sour, you stink, and when you aren't feeling well, you can hardly bubble."

"May I take my favorite spoon from home with me?"

"Of course you may!"

"Will you stay with me for a little bit once we arrive in Belgium?"

"Sure! We could bake something together one last time."

"Yes please! Let's use a recipe that takes a really long time."

FAREWELL

A RECIPE THAT TAKES A REALLY LONG TIME

Saying goodbye was very hard for me, even if I knew that there was no bigger honor for a sourdough than to have its own compartment in the famous Sourdough Library in St. Vith. Vitus was proud, but it was difficult for him to say farewell. He had wished for "a recipe that takes a really long time" for our last joint baking date, and I wanted to find something special for the occasion.

I studied old and new baking books, googled for hours and found numerous recipes. But none of them appeared to be suitable for Vitus's farewell. I needed a recipe in which Vitus could prove what he had in him. A recipe that would not only give us the chance to draw out our farewell but one that also tasted good.

Shortly before our flight home from the US, I went one more time to my favorite baker. I had promised to bring fresh bagels back to Germany. The minute I heard my favorite pastry plop into the bag, I knew what we would bake together.

Back in Munich, I called Karl. "Karl, could we bake bagels before Vitus moves in with you?"

"When are you coming?" asked Karl. "Sure we can do bagels and the compartment in the Sourdough Library is waiting for him."

Up until now I had never dared tackle a bagel recipe. To classify as real bagels, the rings of dough have to be not only baked, but they have to be boiled before-hand, like dumplings. I resolved to ask Karl whether he could help with the baking. Karl is not only the head of all of the wonder-ful sourdough in the Sourdough Library, he is also a brilliant baker!

VITUS'S FAREWELL BAGELS

500 g wheat flour
300 g whole grain wheat flour
16 g salt
16 g sugar
80 g sourdough starter
400 g water

Put all the ingredients into the mixing bowl of the food processor, insert the dough hook and you're ready to start! Knead at medium speed until the dough is smooth and elastic.

Then it needs to rest. Cover the bowl and leave for one hour at room temperature.

Roll the dough into a thick roll and divide into 10 equal-sized pieces. Roll each piece into a sausage about 10 inches long. Flatten one end of each dough sausage and form a ring by using the flattened end to encircle the thick end.

"And why can't you simply make a round ball of dough and make a hole in the middle with your finger?" I asked. "Because that's absolutely not allowed if you want to make a proper bagel," answered Karl firmly.

Cover the rings of dough and leave to stand for 3 hours, after which they are ready for the float test. For the test, a ring is dunked into a bowl of cold water. If it sinks the dough has not risen sufficiently; if it rises, the bagels are ready for the "overnight chilling," as Karl calls it. Bagels like to be cooled well before being bathed in hot water, so they should be put to rest in the refrigerator overnight. Incidentally they can be parked there for up to 3 days before being baked.

After their hibernation, put the bagels into boiling water for one minute. Fish them out with a slatted spoon and lay them on a baking sheet. Bake for 18 minutes at 425°F.

TIP
Cornmeal (polenta) on the baking sheet prevents the bagels from sticking while baking and will make them especially crisp underneath. Bagels can be pepped up with lots of delicious extra ingredients. Roasted onions, spinach, raisins and cinnamon … You can add 150 g of additional ingredients to the amount of dough listed above.

"Vitus, I have to go now!"

"Not yet!"

"But I have to, Vitus."

"Thank you for rubbing my belly so nicely while we were baking bagels."

"It was my pleasure."

"Will Karl really be good to me?"

"I'm positive, Vitus. He's known you since you were a little sourdough. Do you remember?"

"Yes, he said that I should plop out of the jar like applesauce."

"That's right!"

"Did you remember my spoon?"

"I did!"

"Can I keep my jar?"

"No, you're going to be moved into a larger jar and be given a number as well."

"My new jar is going to be very elegant, isn't it"?

"Absolutely! Now you're going to be part of the very prestigious Sourdough Society."

"Are you going now?"

"Yes, but before I do I have to whisper something to you under the lid."

"Something good?"

"Not so loud! Whisper means you have a secret."

"You want to share a secret with me?"

"Yes, while we were baking bagels I removed 50 grams of you."

"Really? I didn't even notice."

"I'm taking the 50 grams home and I'm going to feed them until they bubble again."

"Then I can stay here and at the same time go home with you?"

"Precisely!"

"You're a magician!"

"No, my dear Vitus, you are the magician!"

BYE BYE, VITUS

Vitus now belongs to the Puratos Sourdough Library in St. Vith.
This is the biggest privilege sourdough can receive. They are cooled, stirred and regularly fed there. Bakers the whole world over travel to the Library and scientists visit to research the fermentation of the different kinds of dough.
Karl De Smedt collected the sourdough from around the globe. Some are more than 100 years old, others relatively fresh. But every jar of dough tells a special story.

I'm proud of Vitus.
He grew up with each feeding. In the meantime, his talent amazes even experienced bakers.
Every person we met along the way charged him up with a new story. There was Stefan, for example, who woke an abbey bakery out of its sleeping beauty slumber, and Pablo, who was brought back onto the straight and narrow thanks to sourdough. Then Vanessa's story, in which she exchanged Porsche and Prada for sourdough, and John from Holland, who escaped the tortuous monotony of his life with the help of sourdough. The stories of Josef and those of Stefan, Anil and Lais are embedded deep in Vitus's air bubbles. As is Barbara from Stockholm's life story as well. Then there was the unflappable Patricia, and John and his Brazilian street children. Not to forget Johanna and her daughters … and a little bit of my own story is also in there!

By the way, sourdough generally can't speak.
But one day it happened to Vitus. I was so fascinated with how life was formed out of flour, water and patience that I couldn't help but give him a voice. Shortly afterwards, I even gave him a name because I wanted to address him. I learned a lot from Vitus. Especially patience! And I came to understand that sourdough is not a soulless baking agent. Sourdough is a helpful and friendly living organism, which loves to live in refrigerators and is capable of making people happy … as long as you understand their language.

puratossourdoughlibrary.com

SAYING THANK YOU …

A page plan is made when a book is put together.
Table of contents, chapters, index, copyright page and a corner for the acknowledgements, in which some names are listed one after the other. In writing this book, I left plenty of space right from the very start to show my gratitude. "What kinds of things do you want to write about?" I was asked. "I don't know yet!" I answered. "I can't say at the beginning who I want to thank at the end." In hindsight I know that it was a pretty clever idea. Because now I don't have to be sparing with my acknowledgements due to lack of space but can share them with a full heart.

My biggest thanks go to Puratos, which—for many months—placed their entire knowledge about sourdough and bread baking at my disposal.
Puratos manufactures everything bakers and pastry chefs need for their baked goods. It is a huge company whose cause is to save sourdough from dying out. I was excited about each of my trips to the company headquarters in Groot Bijgaarden near Brussels. Everytime I visited the Puratos Sourdough Library in St. Vith for my research, I learned something new and amazing about sourdough. My work was constantly accompanied by a pleasant aroma. The fragrance of fresh crusts was everywhere and I was allowed to nourish myself from the bakery bread shelves once my work was done.

Stefan Cappelle's and Karl De Smedt's impressive knowledge was invaluable.
In my eyes, they are the sourdough heroes at Puratos. There was not one question which they couldn't answer and they are also particularly nice people. Stefan and Karl, I thank you both from the bottom of my heart. Our work together was pure pleasure!

My thanks to Susanne Döring, who speaks so passionately about bread that you immediately develop a craving for a freshly buttered slice.
If I didn't love to write so much, I wouldn't mind taking over her desk. Not only because of the view of the Grand Place, the most beautiful square in Brussels, but because it's her job to attend to all of the varieties of bread in Europe as well as all of the nice bakers. A dream job! I'm so grateful to you Susanne and the AIBI Association for guidance and resources in the making of this book.

I also acknowledge the cooperation of Dr. Thomas Hagen.
I truly envy him his office as well. Although the view out the window is average, it is full to the brim of the most magnificent books, books about everything beautiful. Many were realized under his tutelage, others are at his disposal free of charge, because it is his job to inform himself about the world of literature. At the beginning, he didn't really have any connection to sourdough. But the force of my passion for this topic soon simply bowled him over. He became a sourdough fan page by page and I could even imagine that, in the meantime, he secretly bakes the recipes from the book at home. Thomas, I send you my heartfelt thanks for your support, as well as for the power from DVA and Prestel you provided me with!

And who is responsible for the gorgeous photos and the brilliant layout? Barbara Simon.
Barbara and I have known each other since our days in television and I've been a fan of her photographs for a long time. When I asked her if she would have fun doing the photos and layout for my new book, she laughed and said "I grew up with beautiful books and typefaces. My Dad is a book binder." That was a much better answer than just "Yes!" Barbara, thank you so much for the great photos. I know that it was hard for you to make a selection. Every single page is a testament to the passion you have for your work. I absolutely adored the deliberation and discussions with you over photos, colors, typefaces and layout of the pages. Thank you for the magnificent design. Your father will be proud of you.

I also send my gratitude to Andrea Cobré for her fantastic work in the production of this book, **Nancy Smith** for her wonderful translation and to **Sarah Trenker** for her proof-reading.

I also acknowledge the contribution of Stefan Dümig.
I have been buying our bread from him for years. When I started to bake myself, he was the person I turned to with my very first questions. **I thank him as a representative for all bakers.** For the love which they bake into their bread every day. And because Stefan Dümig loves sourdough just as much as I do, I have immortalized breads from his "Dinkelbäckerei" on the cover.

While we're speaking about the cover …
I bought the cupboard on the title page at auction for one euro. I knew immediately when I saw the photo of it on eBay, that it would be perfect for the cover of my new book. It had been stored in a garage in Baden-Baden and was so warped that you could hardly open and close the doors. Until **Viivika** showed up … She brought along a trunk full of tools and got the cupboard into shape again. When she finished, it was ready for the cover photoshoot. Thank you, Viivika.

I also want to thank **Carmita and Pierre** for the hospitality which warmed my heart every time I was in Belgium for work.

My gratitude goes out to **Bernadette and Nick** for my stays in White Plains and Pennsylvania. After spending those weeks with you both, the last pages nearly wrote themselves and many new ideas were added. I thank you for this inspiration, Bernadette, and especially cherish your friendship with all my heart!

And last but not least with a mother's heart, I thank my son, Tim.
He went through "thick and thin" with me during the first sourdough experiments. Especially through the "thin" period in which the beginner's models were flat and quite hard. My son nibbled his way courageously through them in the hope of better times. Which ultimately arrived as soon as Vitus came into the picture. Thank you for your patience, my son. In love, your Mama.

BITTEN BY THE BAKING BUG?

If you'd like to learn more about sourdough and are looking for practical help, you're in good baker hands with **YouTube.** There are videos available which address every question about baking with sourdough—from pros and hobby bakers. Just type in the search word and watch the respective tutorial!

Furthermore, there are **Facebook groups** in which sourdough bakers can share their passion with like-minded bakers. You can just read the comments or actively take part in the discussions, ask questions and even find new friends.

www.facebook.com/groups/perfectsourdough/
www.facebook.com/groups/bakingbreadathome/
www.facebook.com/groups/Breadmania/
www.facebook.com/groups/universalbread/
www.facebook.com/Breadworks.nl/

Pinterest and **Instagram** are also treasure troves for the sourdough baker, beginners and advanced bakers. The search word Sourdough opens up a myriad of superb sites.

The selection is even larger on the **WorldWideWeb**. Enter a search word and bathe in photos and recipes.
Here is only a small selection:

www.thequestforsourdough.com
www.mydailysourdoughbread.com
www.theperfectloaf.com
www.thebakingnetwork.com
www.breadandcompanatico.com
www.sourdough.co.uk
www.bread-magazine.com
www.thefreshloaf.com

www.beeshamthebaker.com
www.theclevercarrot.com
www.farine-mc.com

Vitus not only won a place in my heart and his own book …
He is also a virtual celebrity in the **Quest for Sourdough by Puratos**. This is truly a great honor.
www.thequestforsourdough.com/blog/vitus

And he even has his own film!

And what's more, he'll appear regularly on my RAUMSEELE Blog …
www.blog.raumseele.de
There is also a "translate" key for different languages.

ASTERISK NOTES

Page 10   *   Because the Sourdough Library is not open to the public, you can take a virtual tour with Karl De Smedt. www.puratossourdoughlibrary.com

Page 13   *   I've collected a selection of particularly beautiful and informative blogs and Facebook groups in the list of links on page 189. This is, however, only a tiny sampling. There are countless more.

Page 19   *   The Abbey is always open to visitors Tuesday—Sunday from 2–4 p.m. Appointments for individual Abbey tours can be arranged by telephone and there are fantastic rooms which can be booked for seminars. Information at olaf.ude@klosterwettenhausen.de

Page 45   *   I especially like Mock Mills. Not only because they are so beautiful. Wolfgang Mock invented them. Healthy mills are his passion. www.wolfgangmock.com/mockmill-100.html

          ** The attachment mills from Mock are smaller but nearly just as powerful. www.wolfgangmock.com/mockmill.html

Page 57   *   I found my favorite enamel pots at flea markets. Old enamel is truly indestructible. The traditional company Riess in Austria still produces robust enamel kitchenware in the good, time-honored way. www.riess.at

          ** My favorite roasting pans are by Le Creuset. They not only help me wonderfully in bread baking, they can also roast and stew—and they also come in friendly colors. www.lecreuset.co.uk/signature-cast-iron-round-casserole/

         *** Stainless steel pots without plastic parts are also good for baking. They are lighter than cast-iron roasting pans, which is an advantage when you take them out of a 500°F oven. www.lecreuset.co.uk/shop-by-material/signature-stainless-steel

Page 75   *   I like traditional companies which have been manufacturing excellent products for generations. Like Güdes from Solingen. www.guede-solingen.de/en/company

Page 92   *   A conversion table can be found at www.thespruce.com/recipe-conversions-486768

Page 113   *   Simone Streicher is a talented quilter and a good friend with a sense of humor. She said that it was a pleasure to make the puppy box as beautiful as possible for the sourdough starter. Here are her instructions. Thank you, Simone! www.simis-atelier.de

Page 124   *   The Museum for Old Techniques in Grimbergen, Belgium is definitely worth a visit. Especially with children. And if you don't have the time, take a virtual tour at www.mot.be/en/

Page 149   *   *Zirbenholzkästen* (Swiss pinewood boxes) are something truly fine. Classically exquisite boxes are produced by a traditional Bavarian company: the Gustav Konrad family. www.holzartikelmanufaktur.de

Page 161   *   In my opinion, KitchenAid's stand mixer is the most beautiful in the world. I would even love them if they clattered and squeaked … but thank goodness, they don't! They run like clockwork. www.kitchenaid.com/countertop-appliances/stand-mixers/

      **   KitchenAid's food processor is nearly even more beautiful. Especially because it provides you with an entire kitchen team … including kneading dough. www.kitchenaid.com/countertop-appliances/food-processors/

Page 170   *   If you would like to support John's Brazilian street children, you'll find lots of information and even a short film about the Ranch on its Facebook page. www.facebook.com/RanchoNovoHorizonteLarDasCriancasEAdolescentes/

Page 175   *   Here are more instructions from my friend Simone. Everything you need to know about sourdough caps can be found at www.simis-atelier.de

All of the portraits I made of Vitus in his jar were taken with a Polaroid camera. I love instant photos. I liked the idea of being able to hold an analog picture of Vitus in my hands at the end of every story as a complement to Barbara's perfect photographs. I currently have them hanging on the bulletin board in my office.

INDEX

© Prestel Verlag,
Munich · London · New York, 2018
A member of Verlagsgruppe
Random House GmbH
Neumarkter Straße 28 · 81673 Munich

© for the texts by Martina Goernemann, 2018
© for the images by Barbara Simon, 2018,
except p. 51 top and bottom left: private
With respect to links in the book, the Publisher
expressly notes that no illegal content was
discernible on the linked sites at the time the
links were included. The Publisher has no
influence at all over the current and future
design, content or authorship of the linked
sites. For this reason, the Publisher expressly
disassociates itself from all content on linked
sites that has been altered since the link was
created and assumes no liability for such content.
The tips and advice contained in this book
have been carefully considered and checked
by both the author and the publisher. Never-

theless, they are no substitute for competent
medical advice or treatment. All the information
in this book is therefore provided without any
warranty or guarantee whatsoever. Liability on
the part of either the author or the publisher for
any personal injury, property damage or financial
loss is also excluded.

Prestel Publishing Ltd.
14-17 Wells Street
London W1T 3PD

Prestel Publishing
900 Broadway, Suite 603
New York, NY 10003

Concept and production: Martina Goernemann
Editorial direction: Thomas Hagen
Translation from the German: Nancy Smith, Munich
Photos and design: Barbara Simon

Production management: Andrea Cobré
Typesetting: ew print & medien service, Würzburg
Separations: Helio Repro, Munich
Printing and binding: Longo AG, Bolzano

Paper: 140 g Amber Graphics

MIX
Paper from
responsible sources
FSC® C023164

Verlagsgruppe Random House FSC® N001967

Printed in Italy
ISBN 978-3-7913-8432-0

www.prestel.com